You and Your
Small Wonder

Other Works by Merle B. Karnes

Early Childhood Enrichment Series
GOAL
    Language Development
    Mathematical Concepts
    Beginning Science
    Beginning Health and Nutrition
Karnes Early Language Activities (GEM)
Learning Language at Home
Creative Games for Learning
Creative Art for Learning
Learning Mathematics Concepts at Home
Small Wonder!
    Level 1: Activities for Baby's First 18 Months
    Level 2: Activities for Toddlers 18-36 Months
You and Your Small Wonder: Activities for Parents
    and Toddlers on the Go

You and Your Small Wonder

Activities for Busy Parents and Babies

Merle B. Karnes

AGS ®
American Guidance Service
Circle Pines, Minnesota 55014

AGS staff participating in the development and production of this publication:

Program Development

Dorothy Chapman, Director
James Wendorf, Senior Coordinating Editor
Marjorie Lisovskis, Assistant Editor

Product Development

David Youngquist, Director
Lynn Rusch, Materials Development Manager
Carol Wagner, Production Manager
Maureen Wilson, Art Director
Sylvia Carsen, Production Artist

Photographs:

Niedorf Photography

Library of Congress Catalog Card Number: 82-71049
ISBN 0-913476-58-7

To Gregory and Sheri,
the wonderful parents of my grandson, Joshua,
who is indeed a "small wonder."

Contents

ACKNOWLEDGMENTS   ix

INTRODUCTION   1

How to Use the Activities   1
Teaching Tips and Guidelines   2
How to Include Brothers and Sisters in Small Wonder Activities   4

HEALTH AND SAFETY   5

Nutrition   5
Baby-Proofing Your Home   6
Poisonous Plants   10
A Word About Child Abuse and Neglect   10

MILESTONES OF DEVELOPMENT   12

Birth to 12 Months   12
12 to 18 Months   14

HOUSEHOLD PLAYTHINGS   16

EDUCATING ON A SHOESTRING   17

RECOMMENDED READINGS   24

ACTIVITIES   27

Just for the Two of You   27
Just for the Fun of It   43
Changing Time   59
Growing with the Grass   73
A Classroom in the Kitchen   85
Chore-time Chums   101
Bathtime Business   117
Shop, Look, and Listen   131
Teaching — Family Style   143

MORE ABOUT SMALL WONDER   157

INDEX OF ACTIVITIES ACCORDING TO PRIMARY SKILLS EMPHASIZED   159

Acknowledgments

Book 1 of *You and Your Small Wonder* is a handbook of activities that complements Level 1 of the *Small Wonder* program. It culminates many years of experience working with parents of infants and with infants themselves. I especially wish to thank the dozens of parents and infants who inspired the book. Their valuable contributions have been incorporated in the activities.

I am indebted to Paula Strong and Barbara Franke, early childhood specialists and themselves mothers of infants, who made major contributions to the writing and field testing of the activities.

I wish to thank Susan S. Aronson, M.D., F.A.A.P., for carefully reviewing the activities for health and safety concerns. Thanks also to Susanne P. Miskiewicz, mother and reading specialist, and to Dr. Marian Houk, day-care director, for reviewing the manuscript and offering valuable suggestions.

I extend my appreciation to the entire staff of AGS for the knowledge, creativity, skills, and encouragement they provided. My thanks to Don Michaelis and his marketing staff for their research endorsing the need for this book, to Maureen Wilson for the page design, and to Carol Freeman for coordinating production. To James Wendorf I am particularly grateful. His meticulous editing of the manuscript and his attention to its format have enhanced the quality of the book. I am likewise appreciative of the encouragement and creative ideas provided by Dorothy Chapman, Director of Program Development. Last but not least, to John Yackel, President of AGS, I express my gratitude for supporting the development of *You and Your Small Wonder*.

Merle B. Karnes, Ed.D.
Professor of Education
Institute for Child Behavior and
Development
University of Illinois, Urbana

Introduction

A newborn infant seems so tiny and helpless! When you lift him,* he can't even support his head. But by the time he is 18 months old, he will have grown by leaps and bounds and learned more than he ever will again. For you and your baby, the months ahead will be busy and exciting. Your baby will thrive on all the attention and encouragement you offer as he learns about himself, his world, and the people around him.

Book 1 of *You and Your Small Wonder* is designed to help you enhance the special ways you play with your baby and teach him. The activities encourage physical, intellectual, and emotional growth as well as language development in children up to 18 months of age. They are based on activities featured in the *Small Wonder* kit, which was carefully field tested in homes, centers, and clinics across the United States.** Like all parents you'd like to know whether your baby is progressing normally and whether you're doing the best you can to encourage him. The information on infant development presented in the following pages will help assure you. In addition, the activities will help you feel confident about encouraging your baby and getting him off to a good start.

Some activities may give you new ideas; others may reinforce what you're already doing with your baby. Because your day is undoubtedly very busy, many of the activities are designed to fit into your everyday schedule. Others are for special moments that you set aside to spend with your little one. All the activities give your baby a chance to learn in a playful atmosphere. They also give you the opportunity to share the formative experiences of his life and to become a better observer of his development.

HOW TO USE THE ACTIVITIES

The *Small Wonder* activities are grouped into nine thematic units. These units feature activities that can be done at a particular time (such as *Changing Time*), or in a special place (such as *A Classroom in the Kitchen*), or with certain people (such as *Teaching — Family Style*). Within a unit there are 15-18 activities arranged by age range; each unit has several activities for babies between birth and 3 months, 3 and 6 months, 6 and 9 months, 9 and 12 months, 12 and 15 months, and 15 and 18 months. If you're looking for something new to do at bathtime with your 7-month-old, all you have to do is turn to the activities for 6-9 month olds in *Bathtime Business*.

Learning how to work a circle puzzle.

---

*The opening sections of *You and Your Small Wonder* alternate in the use of masculine and feminine pronouns. The information presented here applies to boys and girls alike.

**Merle B. Karnes, *Small Wonder! Level 1: Activities for Baby's First 18 Months* (Circle Pines, Minn.: American Guidance Service, 1979). For information about the complete kit, turn to the section entitled *More About Small Wonder*.

1

As you use the *Small Wonder* activities with your child, let the time you spend be easy and relaxing. When you do the activities you are encouraging your baby in his normal development and strengthening the bond between you. To get the most out of the activities, keep in mind the following suggestions:

- Choose activities that are in your child's developmental range. Your baby is a unique person who will develop at his own pace. He might master some tasks before the normal age and he may be a bit slower at other tasks. If your child is a newborn, begin with the birth-3 month activities. If he's older, you might want to start with activities in the age range below his. For example, if he is 6 months old, try some activities in the 3-6 month range. When he masters those activities, go on to his own age range.

- If your baby cannot do a certain activity, put it aside for a day and then try it again. Don't worry if he does not do a certain task right on schedule — he will reach that milestone in his own time. However, if there are many tasks in your child's age range that he cannot perform, it is a good idea to consult his doctor.

- Your baby might do certain types of activities very well. If so, go on to the next age range and choose similar types of activities that are more challenging. (The index of activities at the back of this book will help you choose.) But be careful not to pressure him to try activities that are beyond his ability — he will only become frustrated.

- You will find that your baby has some favorite activities that he enjoys doing over and over, especially games for the bathtub, music activities, storytelling and rhymes, and sand play. These activities are not limited to one age range. As your child grows and does them over and over, he will expand on these favorite activities, so don't put them aside once he masters them.

- Become familiar with an activity before you begin. After reading it, gather any materials required. If you know what you are doing, you and your baby will have more fun playing together.

- Repeat the activity. The first time you present an activity, it may seem too difficult for your baby. Try it two or three times on different days before deciding it is too hard. Don't frustrate your baby by encouraging him with a game or task that's too advanced; but give him several chances to do what you ask or demonstrate.

Your baby will master tasks by practicing them over a period of time. How many times a *Small Wonder* activity will need to be repeated depends on the skills being developed and your baby's unique rate of development.

Even when your baby seems to have learned a skill, he may forget it. He may be concentrating on a new skill, or he may have learned the skill only for the moment. Skills and abilities will become permanent as your baby practices them. Once he masters a task, he will still enjoy doing it again and again — the success he enjoys with one activity may motivate him to try another.

TEACHING TIPS AND GUIDELINES

You have much to offer your baby! Use your imagination to add special touches to an activity, or to extend and vary it. Rely on your special abilities and interests — whether they be musical, artistic, athletic, or other abilities — to make learning an enjoyable experience for your baby. Your enthusiasm, your approach to an activity, and your willingness to try new approaches will affect his level of achievement and the way he feels about himself.

Keep in mind the following teaching tips while using the *Small Wonder* activities. They have helped other mothers, fathers, and caregivers. If your baby has brothers or sisters, you may want to stress these tips to them so that they learn how to play with the baby.

Choose the right time for the activity.
- Your baby needs to be attentive, so do not attempt an activity when he is fussy, sleepy, or distracted.
- Respect your baby's feelings. Do not take him away from another activity he is enjoying to work on the activity of your choice.

Fit the activity to your baby's mood.
- If he is in an active mood, choose an activity that stresses physical skills.
- "Sit-down" tasks and story time are good choices when your baby is quiet or physically tired but alert.

Pouring takes concentration, and skill.

Set the stage for learning.
- Gather all of the necessary materials before beginning an activity.
- Eliminate as many distractions as possible: Put away other toys, turn off the television or radio, and try to occupy your other children with different activities or include them directly in the baby's activity.
- Be enthusiastic! If you come to the activity with energy and interest, your baby will be more responsive.

Praise your baby's efforts as well as his successes.
- A pat, a hug, a smile, or a kiss is an encouraging sign that babies understand.
- Praise your baby immediately after he succeeds or makes a good effort. Babies learn to do things most quickly when praise is given promptly. They need to know when they're on the right track, since they learn so many things by trial and error.
- Give positive but realistic praise for your baby's efforts. If he tries to roll a ball to you but misses you by a yard, it isn't encouraging to say, "That was terrific!" Such praise is meaningless, and it could actually discourage him. Say instead, "That was a good try! Try again."
- Disapproving criticism and physical punishment discourage learning.
- A disapproving or disappointed tone of voice could speak more harshly to your baby than your actual words. What you say and how you say it can build his self-confidence or destroy it.

Finish an activity before your baby tires or loses interest.
- Work for short periods of time (2-3 minutes in many instances), but repeat the activity often. Very gradually increase the amount of time he works on an activity.

- Never force your baby to finish an activity. Attention span and the readiness to do an activity vary from baby to baby and from day to day with the same baby.

HOW TO INCLUDE BROTHERS AND SISTERS IN SMALL WONDER ACTIVITIES

Babies often inspire jealousy in older brothers and sisters. No matter how much you prepare your other children for the new arrival, you cannot *make* them like that little baby who demands so much of your time and attention. On the other hand, your other children might be delighted and adore the baby. However they feel about the new baby in your home, you can use *Small Wonder* activities to help older brothers and sisters become involved with the baby and learn to include him as a member of the family.

When you are preparing a *Small Wonder* activity, ask your other child or children to join in. Depending on age, he or she might assist you in some way or take part in the activity along with the baby. For example, if you are giving the baby a massage, a two-year-old might gently rub some lotion on the baby and a five-year-old can help you massage the baby's body. You could also give the children massages after you finish with the baby. The section entitled *Teaching — Family Style* suggests specific activities you can do with the entire family.

NUTRITION

Nutrition is a very popular and controversial topic these days. "Health foods" are becoming more and more popular, and the word *natural* is used to describe everything from potato chips to ice cream. It can all be very confusing. Yet there are some basics of nutrition that can help you choose foods and plan meals to ensure that your baby eats a healthy and balanced diet.

The Basics of Nutrition

Although *calories* may be a dirty word to mom and dad, your baby needs many calories in proportion to her* body weight in order to stay healthy and grow normally. The term *calorie* refers to the energy-producing value in foods. Everything she does — exercise, play, sleep, and even eat — requires calories. She is probably a good judge of how much food she needs to eat in order to have enough calories for her active life. Don't coax her to continue eating when she has had enough and don't offer her lots of sweets, which are hard for anyone to resist.

Your baby needs to receive her calories from a variety of foods. Once she is weaned, she needs to eat foods from the basic food groups every day. These groups include proteins, starches, sugars, and fats.

Proteins. Your baby's body uses proteins to build body tissue, especially muscles. To grow normally, her body needs *complete* proteins — proteins that contain the eight essential amino acids. Meat, fish, eggs, soybeans, and milk all contain complete proteins. You can combine other foods to form complete proteins — for example, grains (bread, cereal, rice) and legumes

*The opening sections of *You and Your Small Wonder* alternate in the use of masculine and feminine pronouns. The information presented here applies to boys and girls alike.

(peanuts, beans, peas). Such combinations are contained in bean tacos, peanut-butter sandwiches, and casseroles such as rice with peas. When you combine grains or legumes with even small amounts of milk, cheese, or meat, the total protein quality is improved. Such dishes include oatmeal with milk, cheese and noodles, and chicken-and-rice casseroles. Even on a limited budget you can provide your child and the rest of your family with low-cost meals that are high in protein.

Carbohydrates. Carbohydrates provide the body with starches and sugars — the quick-energy foods. Carbohydrates are obtained from grains and tuberous vegetables (potatoes, beets, carrots, turnips, radishes). Grains and tubers also provide the body with roughage to help in digestion.

Fats. Your baby's body uses fats to support and protect her vital organs and to insulate her body from cold. Since fats are digested slowly, they also add staying power to foods; your baby doesn't feel hungry soon after a meal. However, children can't digest fats as well as adults, so don't feed her too many fatty foods. Milk fat, egg yolk (after nine months of age), butter, margarine or peanut butter used as a spread on bread, and fish oils provide adequate fats.

Vitamins and minerals. Vitamins and minerals are the body's protectors. They keep the body tissues healthy and help the organs function normally. The body receives many vitamins and minerals from fruits and vegetables. Proteins, milk, and carbohydrates provide other vitamins and minerals.

Milk. Although your baby's requirements of protein, most vitamins, and iron are less than an adult's, her growing body needs more minerals, calcium, phosphorus, and vitamin D. Fortified whole or skim milk provides all of these latter nutrients.

Snacks. Your baby cannot eat enough at one meal to last her until the next. A cranky, crying baby might need nothing more than a nutritious mid-morning, mid-afternoon, or evening snack to recharge her.

Sugary or starchy snacks start to be digested right away in your baby's mouth, from enzymes in her saliva. These foods are absorbed into the body quickly and give "quick" energy. But this energy is used up quickly and so it doesn't last long. Proteins add "staying power." If you include some protein at snacktime, snack energy will last a lot longer.

Snack foods can be tasty *and* high in food value. Try some of the following combinations of foods: crackers with small pieces of cheese or meat; fresh fruit with some cheese; bland pudding, fruit puddings, or custard; a glass of milk with peanut butter on crackers, or with a peanut-butter or oatmeal cookie. Such snacks as these provide quick energy and some staying power — enough to last until mealtime.

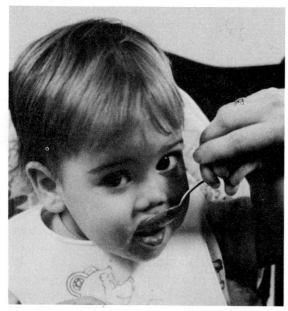

Starting off the day with a nutritious breakfast.

Behavior at Mealtime

Meals can be a problem if you are worried that your baby isn't eating enough or if she will eat only certain foods. At the end of the first year it is normal for a baby's appetite to slow down along with her rate of growth. As long as her favorite food is generally nutritious, there will be no bad effect. To insure that your young child eats a balanced meal, offer small servings of several foods and urge her to eat at least some of each. Then give her more of her favorites.

Whatever you do, try not to let mealtime become a battle of wits between you and your baby. Stay calm. If you fuss over how much she eats or what she eats, she might learn to use mealtime as a way to get attention or gain control over you.

Never use food as a reward for good behavior; nor should you deny your child a meal because of inappropriate behavior. Food is food. If you use it for any other purpose, you are only asking for trouble at mealtime.

While your child is young, you are helping her develop tastes and eating habits that will probably stay with her for life. If you encourage her to eat balanced meals and nutritious foods, you are doing her and her body a big favor.

BABY-PROOFING YOUR HOME

People have probably talked to you about baby-proofing your home. It's true — once your baby can creep or crawl, you will be amazed at what she can get into. Many of the commonplace objects around your house can be hazardous to your curious baby. To protect her from your home, check for and remove household poisons and other hazards — tools, unstable furnishings, cleaning substances, and poisonous plants. Check the quality of toys and make sure the play area of your home is especially safe.

Accidents happen in even the safest households, so be prepared for emergencies. Keep important phone numbers listed near each telephone in your house. List the numbers of your baby's doctor, a nearby hospital emergency room, a poison-control center, an ambulance service, as well as the police and fire departments. When you have a sitter in your home, show that person the list of numbers and write down where you can be reached.

Toys
Toys that are safe for your baby to play with should be made from sturdy, nontoxic materials such as wood, metal, or high-impact plastic. Because of federal regulations, most commercial toys are reasonably safe, especially if you give your baby only those toys that are recommended for her age group. But, particularly in the case of homemade toys, make sure that the paint is lead-free, that wooden toys have no splinters, and that there are no small parts that she can break off easily. Make sure that plastic parts are not combustible and that fabrics and stuffings are not flammable. On stuffed toys, check sewn-on features and fasteners — they should be attached securely.

Play Areas
The following safety checks apply to any area of your home where your baby will be moving around.
- Check the floor for electrical cords on lamps and small appliances. A baby can trip over cords, pull them, or get caught on them, pulling heavy objects onto the floor or onto her head.
- Plug unused electrical outlets with protective safety caps.
- Check tables for sturdiness (even child-size furniture may be unsteady).
- Search the floor periodically for tacks, staples, paper clips, pop tops, pins, or small parts from older children's toys.
- If your child uses a walker, she may have a surprising arm's reach, making more things accessible to her than when she's crawling on the floor.
- Windows that your baby can reach should have locks and restraining bars or adjustable safety catches that can be locked open at a safe width of four inches. Teach your baby not to climb up on window ledges.
- Store toys on sturdy shelves or bookcases that won't collapse or fall over onto your child. If a bookcase is tall and unsteady, anchor it to the wall — once your baby starts climbing, she might find the shelves very inviting.
- A toy chest with a heavy lid should have a catch to hold the box lid open without falling and thereby pinching fingers or hitting your baby's head.
- If you have older children, arrange a play area or a play table for them that is off limits to your baby. Many of their toys are probably dangerous for your baby to play with.

Around the House
- Do not leave such items as cigarettes, tobacco, lighters, dirty ashtrays, matches, and breakables on tabletops that your baby can reach.
- Some tables may have sharp corners and edges. While your baby is learning to walk, you may want to remove the table or cover its corners with fabric.
- Make sure that shelves and drawers that she can reach do not contain dangerous things.
- A tablecloth with a long drop can be tempting to a baby who's learning to pull herself to a standing position.
- Keep containers of liquor, cleaning fluids, perfumes, after shaves, air fresheners, and other toxic substances well out of your baby's reach.
- Keep handbags and purses out of reach.
- Make sure that only lead-free paint is used for painted surfaces throughout your house.

7

In the Kitchen

- Always turn pot handles away from the stove edge so they will be out of your baby's reach.
- Do not let your baby climb onto the stove or the oven door — she could manipulate the knobs and turn on the gas or electricity.
- Keep matches out of reach.
- Cupboards and drawers containing knives or dangerous or breakable kitchen equipment should have childproof secondary latches. These devices are available at hardware stores and are easily installed.
- Install safety catches on all drawers so your baby cannot pull them all the way out.

A safe — and entertaining — kitchen cabinet.

- Keep cleaning supplies out of your baby's reach in an overhead cupboard or in a cupboard fitted with a safety latch. Never keep cleaning agents, waxes, salves, disinfectants, dyes, or bleaches under the sink.
- Always leave labels on containers. Clearly label containers if you transfer something into them for convenience.

In the Bathroom

Your bathroom is probably filled with poisons. These poisons don't look poisonous because they are usually in the form of medication.

- For safety's sake, use childproof safety latches on medicine cabinets and vanity drawers.
- Never leave medicines or vitamins within a child's reach.
- Avoid taking medicine in front of children.
- Throw away unused prescriptions.
- Never give medicine in the dark — you might accidently give the wrong medication or dosage.
- Use a rubber mat or appliques on the bottom of the tub or shower to prevent accidental slipping. Grab bars will provide extra safety.
- Mark hot and cold taps clearly.
- To prevent scalds in the tub, run cold water before hot and then run some cold water to cool off metal fixtures. Set your water heater at 120° F. Once your baby discovers the water taps, she will probably try to turn them herself.
- Put away small electrical appliances like hair dryers, sunlamps, shavers, and electric toothbrushes as soon as you're finished with them.

Stairways

- Do not let your child climb on the kind of open risers often found in basements. She could slip between the risers.
- Openings below a handrail should be blocked by a solid panel or by balusters so your baby can't climb or slip through. Arrange balusters vertically to discourage climbing. Space them only 3-1/2" apart so her head will not get wedged between them.
- You may want to use gates at the top and bottom of staircases in your home. However, a determined baby might soon learn how to squeeze under or climb over a gate.

Storage Areas

- Store boxes and loose items in safe, closed areas.
- If possible, store bikes or baby carriages on the ground floor so that you won't have to carry them up and down stairs.
- Maintenance equipment, such as hedge trimmers, mowers, and rakes, should be kept away from children, preferably in locked cabinets or rooms.
- Hand tools and power tools should also be stored out of reach in a locked place. When using power tools, never leave them running or plugged in if the baby is nearby.
- Safely store gas cans, fertilizers, herbicides, plant food, rat or rodent killers, kerosene, laundry aids, and oils. Take extra precautions when using them near children of any age.
- Make sure that doors on closets have knobs on both sides so that your baby will not be trapped inside.

Take time to enjoy quiet moments.

Outdoors

- If possible, choose a play area for your baby that is away from a street or parking area. A play area adjoining a street should have guard rails, a fence, or other barriers.
- Make sure you can see your baby while she is in the play area. Always supervise her outdoors to avoid accidents and to prevent her from wandering away.
- Check the grounds for broken glass, pop tops, rusted metal objects, and other hazards — especially if your child will be going barefoot.
- Choose a play area that is partially shaded during the day, or take other precautions against a hot summer sun.
- Choose toys for use outdoors that are appropriate to the child's age. A scooter, for example, should fit the size of the child who rides it. It can be dangerous to choose a toy that the baby will "grow into."
- Keep in mind that loose or long clothing can get caught in wheels and spokes.
- Do not leave a wading pool filled with water unless it is covered with a heavy board.
- Let the sun and rain purify sandboxes; don't cover them with sheets of plastic or canvas. A cover of wire netting or window screening will let in air and keep out animals.
- Make sure that wooden equipment has rounded edges to prevent injuries.
- Heavy play equipment should be sunk in concrete deep enough so that it won't pull out of the ground.
- Check equipment for nontoxic finishes and for sturdiness. Now and then, check for sharp edges, loose parts, and rusted areas.
- Sand or grass under slides and other equipment will cushion a fall.
- Teach your baby not to push and shove on play equipment.
- To ensure safety, maintain equipment each season.

POISONOUS PLANTS

Plants are beautiful, but they may be harmful to your baby if she eats any part of them. Some house and garden plants are fatal. As a general rule, keep houseplants out of your baby's reach and check to see if any plants in or around her outdoor play area are poisonous.

Garden plants that have fatal effects include castor beans, laurels, rhododendron, azaleas, and the berries from daphne plants, yew plants, and mistletoe. Wild plants that may cause death include nightshade and hemlock plants, and the berries from moonseed plants. Houseplants that cause fatalities include the seeds of rosary peas and the leaves from poinsettias.

Household plants with poisonous effects include the dieffenbachia and elephant ears.

Some parts of fruit and vegetable plants are poisonous — the leaves of rhubarbs, the foliage and vine of both tomato and potato plants, the twigs of cherry trees, and the leaves of peach trees.

Several types of shade trees have poisonous parts — the acorns and foliage of oak trees; the shoots, leaves, and bark of elderberry and black walnut trees; and the seedpods from golden chain trees.

Many beautiful flowering plants have poisonous parts — the bulbs of hyacinths, narcissus, and daffodils; the leaves and branches of oleanders; the leaves of foxgloves; the young plants and seeds of larkspurs; the leaves of lily-of-the-valley; all parts of the buttercup and the jack-in-the-pulpit.

If your child eats a poisonous plant, induce vomiting and obtain medical treatment immediately. For more information about dangerous plants, contact the poison-control center in your area.

A WORD ABOUT CHILD ABUSE AND NEGLECT

A baby is cute and cuddly, and she inspires strong feelings of maternity or paternity. But a baby can also be colicky and demanding — she can wear a parent out both physically and emotionally. Most people face the demands of parenthood in a healthy and loving manner. However, many parents cannot cope with the stresses their children cause — and the result is often child abuse.

Child abuse is a widespread problem that occurs in households from all socioeconomic groups. Although child abuse and neglect are not normal, they affect normal people — a person does not have to be mentally ill to be a child abuser.

In addition to physically abusing their children, parents can neglect their children by not giving them the love and attention they need or by failing to feed and clothe them properly. Sexual abuse of children is widespread.

Potential abusers include people who were themselves emotionally neglected or physically abused as children, people under severe stress, and people who lack a sense of their own worth. People who are dependent on alcohol or drugs run a higher risk of neglecting or abusing their children than those who are not. Ignorance can create the conditions for child abuse — ignorance of the way a child develops or of the special needs of a handicapped child.

If you are worried that you might abuse or neglect your infant — in any of the ways just described — talk with someone who understands. Call your county's Public Health Nursing Services or Department of Social Services for help. For further information, write to Parents Anonymous, an organization whose sole purpose is to help parents who have abused or neglected their children or who fear they might. The national address is 22330 Hawthorne Blvd. #208, Torrance, CA 90505. Phone (213) 371-3501.

Milestones of Development

During the first year, a baby matures both physically and mentally at a dramatic rate. Never again will you see such rapid change.

Although every baby is unique, all babies change physically and mentally in similar ways. The following guidelines indicate some important developmental behaviors and the age at which they normally occur. The guidelines are *approximate*. No two babies learn to walk or smile or talk at the same age. Babies develop at varying rates within a normal range. One baby may talk at 12 months and yet not walk until he's 15 months old; another normal baby may walk at 9 months but not begin to talk until he's well over a year old. If you see that your baby is developing slowly in several areas, it is a good idea to consult his physician.

BIRTH TO 12 MONTHS

Birth to 1 Month
- Sleeps most of the day and night.
- Shows reflexive movements. For example, when cheek is touched, he turns to that side; when ear is touched, he turns away; when he hears an unexpected noise, his arms and legs extend and retract rapidly.
- Clenches fingers tightly most of the time.
- Thrusts arms and legs in play.
- Lifts head briefly and adjusts body position when held against your shoulder.
- Becomes quiet when held.
- Responds to the sound of a rattle or bell by becoming quiet or moving whole body.
- Cries and makes some throaty sounds.

1 Month
- Presses down on feet and may "step" reflexively if held in a standing position on a firm surface.
- Looks at faces briefly.
- Looks toward a light.
- Usually stops crying when held.
- Cries or is startled when hearing unexpected noises.
- Becomes quiet when hearing a voice.
- Cries when wet or hungry.
- Makes occasional throaty noises.

2 Months
- Holds head at midline when lying on back.
- Lifts head when placed on stomach.
- Rolls from side to back.
- Often clasps hands together.
- Holds a rattle briefly.
- Glances from one thing to another.
- Smiles when someone smiles at him.
- Squeals, coos, and laughs.

3 Months
- Kicks legs actively in a bicycle motion.
- Rolls from stomach to back.
- Holds head erect and steady when held in a sitting position.
- Keeps fingers unclenched when arms are at rest.
- Grasps a small object (a 1" block) between palm and fingers.
- Grasps and holds on to a rattle, and shakes a rattle.
- Looks at fingers and hands.
- Sucks thumb.
- Brings things to mouth.
- Turns head toward sounds or voices.
- Laughs or coos when happy.

4 Months
- Turns from back to side.
- Supports head and chest with arms while lying on stomach.
- Plays with fingers.
- Switches an object from one hand to the other.
- Follows moving things with eyes.
- Reaches out with both hands for items within sight.

- "Helps" while being pulled to a sitting position (his head doesn't fall backward).
- Laughs, coos, cries, gurgles, and "talks" to people and toys.

5 Months

- Rolls from back to stomach.
- Sits briefly without support.
- Sits with support for up to 30 minutes.
- Bounces when held in a standing position.
- Attempts to pick up a small object by raking the table or floor.
- Uses hands to put food into mouth.
- Plays peek-a-boo.
- Enjoys looking at reflection in mirror.
- Smiles spontaneously at people.
- Imitates facial expressions.
- Recognizes family members.
- Makes sounds to entertain himself and "talks" to toys.
- Makes a variety of sounds. For example, *b, m, d, l, n, ah, ee,* and *oo.*
- Recognizes own name.

6 Months

- Raises head while lying on back.
- Grabs and plays with feet.
- Sits briefly without support.
- Reaches out with one hand for something he wants.
- Grasps a tiny object between thumb and opposing fingers.
- Drops things on purpose.
- Transfers items from one hand to the other.
- Plays with objects by banging them on hard surfaces.
- Looks down for objects that have been dropped.
- Drinks from a cup with assistance.
- Makes a variety of sounds. For example, *f, v, th, s, sh, z, m, n, b, d, l, ee, oh, ah,* and *oo.*
- Imitates some sounds you make.
- Coos, gurgles, squeals, laughs, chuckles, grunts, and growls to express pleasure and displeasure.

7 Months

- Rocks when on hands and knees.
- Sits without support for longer periods of time.
- Gets into a sitting position.
- Pulls up to a standing position.
- Holds two small things, one in each hand.
- Enjoys picking up objects and putting them into mouth.
- Makes sounds by combining consonants and vowels. For example, *bababa, mamama,* and *deedeedee.*

8 Months

- Pivots body while lying on stomach.
- Gets into a sitting position.
- Picks up small objects using thumb and index finger.
- Pokes with fingers.
- Makes noise with objects on purpose. For example, he bangs pots and pans.
- Shows fear of strangers.
- Bites and chews.
- Responds to "Hi!"
- Babbles as if speaking a sentence or asking a question.
- Imitates your mouth movements.

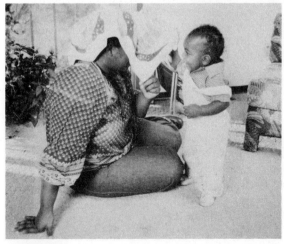

Peek-a-boo!

9 Months

- Starts to crawl.
- Sits without support.
- Stands by holding on to furniture, but does not know how to get down.
- Investigates contents of a container.
- Holds out a toy to another person but will not share it.
- Responds to "No."
- Shrieks to get attention.
- Babbles by combining consonants and vowels, "talks" to himself and others, imitates the speech sounds you make.

10 Months

- Crawls.
- Uses an extended finger to explore and poke small objects.
- Places things in a container. For example, he puts a block or a raisin into a cup.
- Tries to scribble.
- Looks at pictures in books.
- Understands the meaning of some words (*no, mama*) and some directions ("Give it to me").
- Starts to make arm and hand gestures. For example, he waves bye-bye and plays pat-a-cake.
- Repeats speech sounds. For example, *ma-ma, da-da, bye-bye*.

11 Months

- Stands alone briefly.
- Walks by holding on to furniture.
- Attempts to roll or throw a ball back to another person.
- Babbles long utterances that may contain words.
- May speak a few words. For example, *mama, dada, no-no*.

12 TO 18 MONTHS

Between 12 and 18 months of age, babies develop at greatly varying rates, so it is difficult to predict exactly when a baby will acquire a particular skill. The developmental guidelines for this age range are presented in 3-month intervals to allow for the varying rates of development.

12-15 Months

- Gets into a sitting position and sits unsupported for an indefinite period of time.
- Pulls up to a standing position and gets down.
- Stands without support.
- Walks sideways while holding on to furniture; walks forward while holding an adult's hand; starts to take independent steps.
- Throws and rolls a ball.
- Plays with toys by manipulating them.
- Stacks objects two-high.
- Scribbles.
- Turns the pages of a book.
- Shows a variety of emotions, including possessiveness, jealousy, anxiety, and affection.
- Drinks from a cup.
- Eats with hands and attempts to use a spoon.
- Helps pull off clothing.
- Pays attention for longer periods of time and shows an interest in surroundings.
- Increases spoken vocabulary to as many as six words in addition to *mama* or *dada*; babbles long utterances; imitates sounds, parts of words, and words; sings as if speaking sentences; understands many familiar words and simple directions; makes such animal sounds as *meow, woof-woof,* and *moo.*

15-18 Months

- Walks steadily.
- Walks down stairs, up stairs, and backwards.
- Attempts to run.
- Plays with toys purposefully.
- Stacks three or four objects.
- Helps to get dressed. For example, he raises arms, offers foot, puts on hat,

Learning speech sounds.

and pulls off socks.
- Uses a cup and spoon fairly well.
- Starts to see the difference between foods and nonfoods.
- Understands many words and directions.
- Points at familiar objects when asked to.
- Points to body parts (eyes, nose, mouth, feet, and stomach).
- Indicates what he wants by pointing or patting and by making sounds.
- Increases spoken vocabulary to as many as 12 words; babbles long utterances.

Household Playthings

Many commercially made toys make fine playthings, but there's no guarantee your baby will like them. It can be frustrating to see your child ignore an expensive toy! You can avoid the expense and frustration by using items you already have at home. There are many things around your house that can become safe, fascinating toys for your baby. And if she puts any of these aside, you can retrieve them for your own use. Here's a list of items with their uses:

- *Old-fashioned wooden clothespins and a loaf pan.* The baby picks up clothespins and puts them into the pan; later on, as a toddler, she may be able to push the clothespins onto the edge of the pan.
- *Clothespins and an empty coffee can with a taped rim.* The baby drops the pins into the can.
- *Pots and pans with fitted lids.* The baby fits the lids onto the pans or bangs the lids together.
- *Sets of measuring spoons or cups.* The baby stacks the spoons or cups.
- *Cans of various sizes.* The baby stacks the cans or arranges them in a "nest."
- *Muffin tins.* The baby puts small objects into the individual cups.
- *Soft plastic bottles.* The baby kicks, rolls, or squeezes the bottles. They can be made into rattles by putting small objects inside and covering the top securely.
- *Coffee percolator parts.* The baby puts the coffee pot together.
- *Empty milk cartons.* The baby uses the cartons as building blocks.
- *Unbreakable mirrors.* The baby looks in the mirror, recognizes herself, and plays peek-a-boo.
- *Oatmeal boxes.* The baby puts things into the boxes and takes them out. She stacks them.
- *Plastic jars and jar lids.* The baby removes and replaces the lids.
- *Magazine pictures.* The baby names people, things, and activities.
- *Items of clothing.* The baby names the clothing, matches clothing to body parts, and helps you dress her.
- *Unbreakable plastic dishes, cups, or coasters.* The baby stacks the objects.
- *Two- or three-piece puzzles made from magazine pictures glued onto cardboard.* The baby fits the pieces together.
- *Empty spools of thread.* The baby stacks or rolls the spools, or puts them into a container. She puts a string through them.
- *Empty boxes.* The baby crawls through a large box whose ends have been removed, stacks small boxes, and opens and closes boxes with lids.
- *Cardboard tubes from toilet tissue and paper towels..* The baby rolls the tubes, looks through them, and makes sounds into them.
- *Cottage cheese or margarine containers.* The baby stacks the containers and uses them as rattles when small objects have been placed inside.
- *Wooden spoons.* The baby bangs the spoon against pots and pans.

A new friend?

Educating on a Shoestring

If you have some spare moments in your busy day, you can put together simple and inexpensive toys for your child to use. Following are directions for making different playthings and ideas on how to introduce these homemade toys to your baby. An appropriate age range is given for each plaything. When you put together a toy, keep in mind the safety hints suggested in the "Toys" section of *Health and Safety*.

Jumping Jack Clown *(Birth-3 months)*
During the baby's first few weeks, he will usually lie with his head turned to one side. So hang this jumping jack on the side of his crib, where he can study it carefully.

To make the clown you will need five paper fasteners (available in stationery stores), cardboard, crayons, nontoxic paste, and scissors. You will also need gift-wrap paper with a lively pattern (bold designs fascinate infants).

First, cut out cardboard body parts for your clown. Cut a circle for the head, a triangle for a hat, an oval for the body, and four long, narrow rectangles for arms and legs. Trace all the cardboard pieces, except the circle, on the gift-wrap paper. Cut out these paper body parts and paste them onto the corresponding cardboard pieces. Then draw a happy clown face on the cardboard circle and paste the triangle hat onto the clown's head. To assemble the clown, use the paper fasteners to join all the parts together.

Hold the clown in front of your baby's face and shake it so that its body jiggles. Then tape the clown to a wall next to your baby's crib so that he can see the lively patterns and the smiley clown face.*

---
*Do not leave wrapping paper within the baby's reach. Such paper is made of toxic materials that should not be put in the mouth.

Marvelous Mobile *(Birth-3 months)*
Mobiles make wonderful toys for babies' first few months. They will be fascinated by the bright colors and intriguing shapes.

You will need two drinking straws, two rubber bands, string, and eight or more colorful lightweight objects. These might include a napkin ring, a plastic cookie cutter, a comb, a plastic spoon, a large button (larger than 1" diameter), an artificial flower, a plastic measuring cup, and a fancy key holder. (You can create an especially attractive mobile using wooden Christmas tree ornaments.)

To construct the mobile, make an X with the two drinking straws. Then wrap the rubber bands around the straws at the point where they intersect. They should stay together in the X-shape.

Cut pieces of string about 12" long. Tie one end of each string to an object. Tie the other end around one of the straws. Arrange the strings so that there are at least four objects hanging from each straw. Tie a long string around the point where the straws intersect. Hang the finished mobile from the ceiling above your baby's crib, changing table, or playpen.

Marbles in a Jar *(Birth-3 months)*
A baby who begins to reach toward objects and bat them with a fist will be fascinated with a jar of marbles. For several weeks this may be his favorite plaything.

You will need a small, clear plastic jar with a lid, and enough marbles to fill the jar halfway. (You can substitute nuts and bolts or screws for the marbles. But colorful marbles are more fun for your baby to look at.)

Fill the jar halfway with the marbles. Then twist on the cap and *make sure* that it is tightly secured. (It is dangerous for babies to handle such small objects.) Place the jar on its side on the floor. Lay your baby on his back next to the jar and turn his head toward it. Roll the jar slightly so that the marbles rattle and attract his attention.

This toy is appropriate only for a few weeks. As soon as your baby can grab the jar and hold it, remove this breakable plaything from his toy collection.

Jingle Roll (*Birth-3 months*)
Babies like to look at things, make them move, and listen to the sounds they produce. You can create a toy that jingles when it swings or rolls.

This toy is very easy to make. You will need an empty toilet-paper roll, masking tape, and a large jingle bell (larger than 1" diameter). Cover one end of the toilet-paper roll with tape. Then drop the jingle bell inside and tape the other end shut.

To use this as a hanging toy, tape string to the toilet-paper roll and hang it over your baby's infant seat or crib. He can reach toward the toy and bat it with a fist. He will enjoy watching it swing and listening to the jingle of the bell inside.

To use the toy on the floor, lay your baby on his tummy or back. Place the toy next to him so he can hit it with a fist to make the toy roll and jingle.

Be sure to remove the toy once your infant can grab hold of it and starts putting it into his mouth.

Bumpy Balls (*3-6 months*)
Here, at last, is a way to put old socks to good use. You can make them into "bumpy balls" for your baby to handle and examine.

You will need several old socks and lots of small objects, such as coins, marbles, poker chips, dried beans, shredded foam, or empty thread spools. Since you will put

the small objects into the socks, mend any holes in them. Then fill a sock halfway with several things and tie the open end of the sock into a knot. For extra safety, stuff this sock into another one and tie its end into a knot.

Let your baby play freely with the bumpy balls. But as soon as he gets a tooth or two, eliminate them from his toy collection. Otherwise, he might chew a hole in a sock and choke on the tiny things inside.

Learning to sit without help.

Feely Blanket (*3-6 months*)
Introduce your baby to different textures with an attractive feely blanket.

Collect a variety of scrap materials that have different textures: fake fur, terrycloth, satin, broadcloth, wool, polyester, felt, and different wales of corduroy. Cut the fabric into squares of the same size and sew them together by hand or machine to make a patchwork blanket.

Rub the different textures along your baby's arms, legs, and face while you talk to him about the sensations. Once he can hold objects, hand him the feely blanket to examine by himself.

Clatter Hoop *(6-9 months)*
This noisy hoop may become one of your baby's favorite rattles.

To make the hoop you will need several key rings and an embroidery hoop. The hoop can be metal, wood, or plastic, but use only a plain hoop that has no springs, screws, or cork on it. Slip the key rings around the embroidery hoop.

When your baby shakes the hoop, the rings will clatter together and make a wonderful racket. If you have a jumper seat, pin the clatter hoop to the front of the seat with a clean diaper pin. Then he can play with the hoop as he bounces up and down.

String of Spools *(6-9 months)*
Your baby may enjoy playing with a string of empty spools for many months to come. Of course he will use them in different ways as he gets older. Right now he can shake them and study them carefully. Before long he will put them around his neck to wear in pretend play. As he gets older, he'll enjoy putting the spools on the string to make a string of spools.

To make a string of spools, simply put three or four empty spools on a shoestring and tie the ends of the string together. Then give it to your baby.

Water Roll *(6-9 months)*
Now that your baby is able to pick up and hold objects, he will marvel at a water-filled toy that he can shake and examine.

Use a soft, clear plastic jar or bottle that has a screw-on lid, such as a baby bottle, shampoo bottle, or vinegar jar. Find a small brightly colored object and put it into the plastic container. This might be a poker chip, a marble, a plastic thimble, or a small candle. (You may want to put more than one object into the container.) Then fill the jar or bottle with water and screw the lid on tightly.

Hand your baby the toy. As he handles the container, he can watch the objects swirl around in the water. You might also show him how to give the container a push so that it rolls along the floor.

Puppets *(9-12 months)*
Puppets can be made out of paper bags, socks, poster board, construction paper, and empty toilet-paper tubes. Each puppet looks different and can act differently once you give it a voice and a personality.

Paper-Bag Puppet
- Place the paper bag in front of you so the bag is folded flat, with the opening toward you and the bottom faceup.
- Using crayons or felt-tip pens, draw a face on the bottom of the bag, putting the mouth where the bottom folds over the side of the bag. Slip your hand and arm into the bag to make the puppet's mouth move and "talk."

Sock Puppet
- Sew buttons (larger than 1" diameter) on the toe of a sock for eyes, nose, and mouth. Or paint and draw them on. Yarn can be used for hair. Cloth scraps, rick-rack, and lace can be added to "dress up" the puppet.

- Slip the puppet onto your hand and make it come to life. Or stuff the sock with old rags or newspaper. Then push a stick or ruler into the puppet and tie a string around the opening of the sock to hold the stick in place. Hold the stick and bounce the puppet up and down as it talks.

Stick Puppet
- Draw an animal or person on poster board. Draw or paste on a face and other features. Cut out the figure.
- To make a handle, tape a popsicle stick (found in craft stores) or tongue depressor onto the back.

Tube Puppet
- Draw or paste a face and other features onto an empty toilet-paper tube.
- A robe or dress may be added. Cut a slit in the middle of a square piece of fabric. Slip the top of the tube through the slit. Tie string, ribbon, or yarn around the center of the tube to hold the cloth in place.
- To make a handle, tape a popsicle stick or tongue depressor inside the tube.

Construction-Paper Finger Puppet
- Draw a semicircle on a piece of paper. Then cut out the shape.
- Bend the two corners toward each other, overlapping them to form a cone. Tape the edges together.
- Draw a face and clothing on the cone and add yarn "hair."

Bean Bags *(9-12 months)*
Bean bags are easy to make and can be used in a variety of ways. They can be thrown, caught, or stacked. If you make the bean bags out of different fabrics, your baby can also learn about textures and colors. Sometimes they are fun just to squeeze!

Puppets can spark a young child's imagination.

For each bean bag you will need two 7" squares of fabric and one cup of navy beans. To make a larger or a smaller bean bag, begin with a larger or a smaller square. Of course, a larger bag will need more beans and a smaller bag fewer beans.

- Place one fabric square on an ironing board, with the finished side down. Fold one edge of the square 1/2" toward the inside of the fabric. Iron the fold. Repeat with the other fabric square.
- Put one square on top of the other so the folded edges are aligned and the finished sides of the fabric are together. Stitch around three sides, 1/2" from the edges. Do not stitch around the side that has the folds.
- Sew over the first stitching.
- Turn the bean bag right side out. Pour in the beans and stitch the open edge closed. Then sew over the stitching.

A Custom-Made Book *(12-15 months)*
When you select a book for your baby, keep in mind two things: content and durability. When making a book for your baby, you are the author, so you select the content. If you use a photo album with self-adhesive pages, the book is also

durable. Sticky fingerprints are easy to wipe off the pages, and the content of each page can be changed as your baby tires of it. Use the following ideas to make a book:

- Put only one picture on each page. You can find simple pictures in old catalogs, magazines, calendars, and greeting cards.
- Make a book of items that are very familiar to your baby (for example, toys, a cup, a high chair, a spoon, a dog, a mother, a chair, a crib, a baby). Write the name of each object on a piece of paper and place it under the picture.
- Make a book of colors. Put in pictures of things that are red, or blue, or green, and so forth.
- Make a book of items that "go together." Put in pictures of things to wear, or things to eat, or things to play with.
- Make a book of animals, toys, or plants.
- Place identical pictures on opposite pages. Show your baby the picture on one page and ask him to find a picture just like it on the opposite page: "Here is a teddy bear. Point to the teddy bear on this page."
- Make a book of places your baby has been (for example, a swimming pool, park, restaurant, grandma's house, or a grocery store).
- Make a book of people (happy people, sad people, young people, old people, twins, mothers, fathers). Try to include people from all over the world.

Form Can (*12-15 months*)
This toy encourages your baby to coordinate his eye and hand movements. To make it you will need a knife, a two-pound coffee can, a felt-tip pen, several colorful 2 1/2" balls (these can be purchased in most variety stores), a 3" cardboard circle, and contact paper (optional).

- Place the 3" circle on the plastic lid of the coffee can and trace around it.
- Cut along the outline of the circle, making a hole in the lid.
- Cover the coffee can with contact paper (optional).
- Place the plastic lid on the coffee can.

Show your baby how to drop a ball into the hole. Name the color of each ball as your baby places it in the hole.

Pull Toys (*12-15 months*)
Once babies begin walking, they discover the luxury of having two free hands. Their hands aren't likely to stay empty for long, though. Often as not they will find something they can carry, push, or pull as they journey throughout the house.

Shoe-Box Express
- Make a hole in the center of one end of an empty shoe box.
- Slip a 2' length of cord or rope through the hole and tie a knot on each end of the cord.
- If you wish, decorate the box with contact paper, construction paper, or ribbons.

Your baby now has a wagon in which to carry all his prized possessions.

Oatmeal Surprise
- Put some beans or pebbles into an empty, round oatmeal or cornmeal box.
- Punch a hole in the lid of the box.
- Tie a knot on one end of a 2' length of cord.
- Thread the cord through the lid so the knot is on the inside of the lid.
- Place the lid on the box and tape it securely shut.
- Decorate the box with wrapping paper, construction paper, or contact paper.
- If you have a large wooden bead, place it on the end of the string. Tie a

knot on both sides of the bead so it won't slip down or off the string.

Your baby will enjoy pulling, swinging, and rolling this box, which rattles when it moves.

Playdough for Four *(15-18 months)*
This recipe is easy to make, and the ingredients are things you are likely to have in your kitchen. Keep in mind that it's cheaper to make playdough than to purchase it.

    3 cups flour
    1 cup salt
    1 cup water (approx.)
    Food coloring

- Mix the salt and flour together in a bowl.
- Slowly stir in enough water to moisten the dough.
- Knead the dough, adding more water as needed.
- Divide the dough and shape it into balls. Add a few drops of food coloring to each ball and knead the color into the dough.

If the dough is left out, it will dry. To keep it moist, store it in the refrigerator in a tightly sealed container. Remove the dough from the refrigerator one hour before your child will use it so that it returns to room temperature.

A Square Sponge Puzzle *(15-18 months)*
For this learning toy you will need a plastic sandwich container, nontoxic paste, and sponges and construction paper in yellow, blue, green, and pink (or other colors of your choice).

- Make a square from each color of construction paper about one-quarter the size of the sandwich-box bottom.
- Paste the squares to the inside bottom of the sandwich box.

- Cut out a square from each sponge that is slightly smaller than the construction-paper squares.
- Place the sponge squares on the construction-paper squares of the same color.
- Put the lid on the box.

Give your baby the box and ask him to remove the lid and the sponges. After he is well acquainted with the sponges, show how to put each sponge square on top of a construction-paper square. Don't be concerned about matching colors until your baby is about 18 months. When he is playing with the toy, you can name the shape and color of each sponge.

Coping and caring.

Homemade Finger Paint *(15-18 months)*
Place a dab of homemade finger paint on some paper and help your child swirl the colors into delightful designs. Once he gets the hang of it, he will explore the colors busily all by himself.

    1 envelope unflavored gelatin
    1/4 cup cold water
    1/2 cup cornstarch
    3/4 cup cold water
    2 cups boiling water
    Small screw-top jars

- Add 1/4 cup water to gelatin. Set aside.
- Mix 3/4 cup water with cornstarch in saucepan and stir to a smooth paste.
- Slowly stir boiling water into cornstarch mixture.
- Cook over medium heat. Stir mixture constantly until it boils and is clear.
- Remove from heat. Stir in gelatin.
- Divide into jars.

The paint may be colored with food coloring or a variety of food items you may have on hand. Fruit-drink powders make lovely colors. Soy sauce makes a rich brown paint, mustard a striking yellow, and a little grape juice an attractive purple. The paint can smell as good as it looks if you add an extract such as vanilla, peppermint, lemon, or almond. The paint can be stored in tightly covered containers in the refrigerator for several days.

Homemade Paste (*15-18 months*)
You can purchase nontoxic paste at stores that sell school supplies or art supplies and at many toy stores. However, paste dries out quickly even when it is stored in a sealed container. If you make a very small amount of paste at home, your child will probably use it before it dries up. If he does not use all of it at one sitting, store it in a plastic container in your refrigerator.

> 1/4 cup boiling water
> 1/2 cup flour

- Stir the flour into the boiling water.
- Stir the mixture over a low heat until it appears shiny and thick.

Your young child will probably be as interested in the paste itself as in what he can do with it. Help him explore the paste before you show him how to use it.

Recommended Readings

Braga, J., and Braga, L. *Children and adults: Activities for growing together.* Englewood Cliffs, New Jersey: Prentice-Hall, 1976.

Brazelton, T. *Infants and mothers.* New York: Dell Publishing Co., 1969.

Brazelton, T. *Toddlers and parents: A declaration of independence.* New York: Delacorte Press, 1974.

Caplan, F., ed. *Parents' yellow pages.* Garden City, New York: Anchor Press/Doubleday & Co., 1978.

Caplan, F., and Caplan, T. *The second twelve months of life: A kaleidoscope of growth.* New York: Grosset & Dunlap, 1977.

Dodson, F. *How to parent.* New York: New American Library, 1973.

Dodson, F. *How to father.* New York: New American Library, 1975.

Dreikurs, F., and Soltz, V. *Children: The challenge.* New York: Meredith Press, 1964.

Lansky, V. *The taming of the C.A.N.D.Y. monster.* Wayzata, Minnesota: Meadowbrook Press, 1978.

Levy, J. *The baby exercise book: The first 15 months.* New York: Pantheon, 1975.

Loebl, S., and Als, I., M.D. *Parents Magazines mother's encyclopedia and everyday guide to family health.* New York: Dell Publishing Co., 1981.

Marzollo, J., ed. *9 months, 1 day, 1 year: A guide to pregnancy, birth and baby care, written by parents.* New York: Harper & Row, 1975.

Marzollo, J. *Supertot: Creative learning activities for children from one to three and sympathetic advice for their parents.* New York: Harper & Row, 1977.

McDiarmid, N. J.; Peterson, M. A.; and Sutherland, J. R. *Loving and learning: Interacting with your child from birth to three.* New York: Harcourt Brace Jovanovich, 1975.

Newson, J., and Newson, E. *Toys and playthings.* New York: Pantheon, 1979.

Olness, K., M.D. *Raising happy healthy children.* Wayzata, Minnesota: Meadowbrook Press, 1977.

Princeton Center for Infancy and Early Childhood, Caplan, F., ed. *The first twelve months of life: Your baby's growth month by month.* New York: Grosset & Dunlap, 1971.

Pushaw, D. R. *Teach your child to talk: A parent handbook.* New York: CEBCO Standard Publishing Co., 1976.

Rubin, R. R.; Fisher, J. J., III; and Doering, S. G. *Your toddler: Ages one and two.* New York: Macmillan Publishing Co., 1980.

Watrin, R., and Furfey, P. H. *Learning activities for the young preschool child.* New York: D. Van Nostrand Co., 1978.

White, B. L. *A parent's guide to the first three years.* Englewood Cliffs, New Jersey: Prentice-Hall, 1980.

Just for the Two of You

1. Enjoying a Massage
2. Lifting My Head
3. Looking Around
4. Playing Rhyme Games
5. Rolling Over
6. Exercising
7. Handling Objects
8. Exercising Arms and Legs
9. Pulling to a Stand
10. Stacking Bean Bags
11. Two Games for Two People
12. Crawling After "Wiggly"
13. Dancing Together
14. Playing a Game of "Checkers"
15. Looking at Photographs of Baby
16. Pretending to Talk on the Telephone
17. Enjoying a Book
18. Solving Simple Problems

1. ENJOYING A MASSAGE

Age Range
Birth-3 months

Materials
• None

There will be times when your infant cries and tenses his* body for no apparent reason. Life in the outside world is new and uncertain, and so he may need *special* loving and caressing to help him relax. At these times when your baby seems distressed, a gentle massage may help to soothe and relax him.

If possible, dress the baby only in a diaper. But if the room is chilly, put him in a loose-fitting gown. Then sit on the floor with your legs together. Lay the baby faceup on your outstretched legs with his feet toward your body. First massage his trunk. Starting at his right upper thigh, move the palm of your hand slowly up to his left shoulder. Then move your other hand from his left upper thigh to his right shoulder. Repeat this movement several times. Talk quietly to your baby as you massage his trunk: **"Quiet, (baby's name). Relax your little body. Doesn't that feel good?"** If your infant continues to cry, stop after this massage and try again at another time. It may take a few sessions for him to relax and enjoy this new sensation.

If your baby enjoyed the trunk massage, massage his arms and legs. To massage his right arm, hold his right hand firmly with one hand. Then encircle his right wrist with your other hand and move slowly from his wrist to his shoulder. Repeat this movement several times, always moving from wrist to shoulder. Then do the same with his left arm. To massage each leg,

Infants enjoy having their back massaged, too.

move your hand from his ankle to his upper thigh in the same way that you massaged each arm. Remember to talk in a soft voice to your baby as you stroke his body: **"Oh, so nice. You aren't crying anymore!"** ✖

2. LIFTING MY HEAD

Age Range
Birth-3 months

Materials
• None

Between birth and three months your baby's ability to control her* wobbly head will improve greatly. When you hold your newborn in a sitting position, her heavy head will flop forward or backward on her limp neck. But do the same thing in three months and she will maintain strong control for a minute or longer. Although

*In odd-numbered activities, the baby is referred to as a boy. In even-numbered activities, the baby is referred to as a girl.

*In even-numbered activities, the baby is referred to as a girl. In odd-numbered activities, the baby is referred to as a boy.

head support is a skill your baby will develop on her own, you can have fun helping her practice.

During the first few weeks, encourage your infant to control her head while you hold her upright in your arms. Hold the baby facing you, putting one hand on her upper back. Talk to her and smile so that she raises her head to look at you. She will be able to hold her head steady for a few seconds. If her head flops backward, support it with your hand. Don't worry when your baby's head flops like this while you're supporting her trunk — only vigorous shaking is likely to result in any harm to the infant.

During the second month your baby will begin to hold her head up while lying on her belly. To encourage her, lay your own head on the surface in front of her so that you are at her eye level. Then talk to her so that she notices you. As she looks at your face, raise your head slightly so that she raises hers, too. She will be able to support her head for a few seconds. Reward her with a big smile and lots of sweet talk: **"What a strong baby you are. You can hold your head up."**

During the third month your baby will begin to hold her head steady when you hold her upright. Walk around a room,

A friendly puppet can encourage an infant to look up.

carrying the baby in an upright position with her back resting against your chest. Look to see if some object catches her attention. Move so that the object is slightly behind her — she may try to raise her head to look at it. ✖

3. LOOKING AROUND

Age Range
Birth-3 months

Materials
• Household objects

Babies love to be cuddled and carried. In fact, there will be times when your infant refuses to let you put him down. Sometimes this happens when he is tired or colicky, but often he just wants to be held. If your baby seems to be relaxed and alert while you are holding him, share this time together by walking and talking to him.

Carry your baby in your arms while you take him on a tour of your house or an outdoor area. Hold him upright — facing away from you — so that you can look at things together. (You may want to use a carrier pack.) As you walk, describe anything that catches his eye: **"That's the toaster. See how shiny it is. When we put bread in the toaster, it gets hot."** Although your baby can't understand you now, over time he will begin to understand that you're communicating with him.

Your baby will especially enjoy looking at things that move. Show him the swaying pendulum on a clock, a fluttering curtain, the whirling blade on a fan, the action on a TV screen, or the fish swimming in an aquarium. If he is very interested in something, he may be content to sit in an infant seat and watch it for a while, while you take a breather. ✖

4. PLAYING RHYME GAMES

Age Range
3-6 months

Materials
• None

Your baby is probably very sociable by now. Most young babies enjoy company and insist on quite a bit of attention during their waking hours. Action rhymes offer a delightful way to entertain your baby during special moments. Try the following rhymes, or others that you remember from your own childhood.

Lay the baby on her back, facing you. Then say the following rhyme and perform the actions as you recite the words:

> *I squeeze (baby's name) fingers,*
> *I wiggle (baby's name) toes,*
> *I give (baby's name) a great big hug,*
> *And kiss her little nose.*

Gently bounce the baby on your lap while you say this next rhyme. Hold her securely around her waist or chest (not by the upper arms) while you bounce her. If your baby's head wobbles limply as she goes up and down, save this rhyme until she can control her head steadily:

> *Clip-clop, clip-clop,*
> *Goes the little horse.*
> *Here and there and everywhere,*
> *And back again, of course.*

The following rhyme is a finger play. Wiggle a different finger on your baby's hand as you say each line in the verse. When you say the last line, run your fingers up and down her arm:

> *This little mouse eats corn all day.*
> *This little mouse plays in the hay.*
> *This little mouse says squeak, squeak, squeak.*
> *This little mouse digs holes by the creek.*
> *This little mouse goes up and down,*
> *Up and down, 'round the town.*

A game of "Where Is Thumbkin?"

Be creative! Make up your own rhymes — about members of the family, pets, favorite activities . . . even the weather. Your baby will love the sound and rhythm of your voice. ✖

5. ROLLING OVER

Age Range
3-6 months

Materials
• None

Your baby will eventually roll over on his own, but he may enjoy learning how to do it with help from you. Most babies roll from stomach to back before they can go from back to stomach. If you help your baby practice both skills, he can decide which to do first. Keep in mind: even though your baby can't roll over by himself, he can wiggle his way to an edge quite easily. Do not leave him alone on a bed, couch, or other surface without at least a 12" high barrier around him. (Pillows are not enough.)

To roll from stomach to back, place your baby on his belly. Then place his right arm down along his right side. Gently push him over by lifting his left hip toward his right side. After he gets the hang of it, push him from his belly to his side and see if he will roll the rest of the way himself. Praise him lavishly if he does: **"You did it! What a good job!"** Eventually your baby will roll from stomach to back when you lift his hip slightly. Remember to help him practice rolling toward both the right and the left side.

Rolling from stomach to back.

To roll from back to stomach, lay your baby on a firm surface such as a carpeted floor, a bed, or his crib. Hold the back of his right thigh with your left hand, and use your right hand to extend his left arm up alongside his head. Push him over toward his left side with your left hand. Once he's on his side, he may push himself the rest of the way. Be very careful to keep his left arm extended up as he rolls so that he doesn't hurt his shoulder or arm. Remember to congratulate your baby and give him a big kiss: **"You rolled over! Wasn't that exciting?"** 🧍

6. EXERCISING

Age Range
3-6 months

Materials
• None

Both you and your baby can benefit from the following exercise because you do it together. Not only will you improve your bodies, you will also share some special moments.

Dress both yourself and your infant in comfortable clothing that leaves you free to move. Then lie on your back on a carpeted floor or a rug. Raise your knees to your chest and place your baby on your shins so that the two of you are face to face. (It might be easier if you have someone else put the baby on your legs for you.) Hold your baby's bottom so that she doesn't slide off your shins. She should be able to hold her head steady as she peeks over your knees. If she cannot, put her down and try this exercise again when your baby has more head control. If your little one holds her head up well, talk to her for a while: **"Hello up there. How did you get on my legs?"**

Then while you are holding her bottom, raise and lower your feet so that the baby moves up and down. If she enjoys the ride and maintains good head control, inch her body forward a little until her shoulders extend beyond your knees. Give her another ride up and down and then put her down so that she doesn't become overtired. Repeat this exercise at other times, inching her forward each time. Eventually she should hold herself steady while her chest extends past your knees. This exercise will strengthen the baby's neck, arms, shoulders, and chest. It will help you firm up your legs and bottom. 🧍

7. HANDLING OBJECTS

Age Range
6-9 months

Materials
• 3 toys small enough to hold (larger than 1" diameter)

Babies enjoy holding objects and exploring them with their hands. They learn about them this way — their shapes, sizes, weights, and the sounds they make. They also learn about their own body and the things they can do with it. You can use some simple toys to help your baby as he learns more about his hands and how to use them.

Hand your baby one of the toys. While he is holding the toy in one hand, place his other hand on it, too. Help him let go of the toy with the first hand and hold it with the other one. Then congratulate him: **"You switched the toy. Good job!"** Babies

generally learn the skill of transferring an item from one hand to the other around five or six months.

Make the game more challenging by using three toys. Give your baby a toy to hold in each hand. Then show him a third toy and see if he will drop one or both of the toys in order to grab the third one. If not, jiggle the toy and talk to him encouragingly: **"Here's a noisy rattle. Would you like to hold it?"** Your baby may become frustrated as he holds the first two toys and watches the third one longingly. If so, take a toy out of one of his hands and give him the third toy. As your baby develops, he will eventually learn how to drop a toy so that he can grab another one.

Let your baby work on these activities on his own while strapped into his car seat during outings. You can keep the toys within his reach by tying them to his seat with string. 🧒

8. EXERCISING ARMS AND LEGS

Age Range
6-9 months

Materials
• 3 or more favorite toys

Soon your baby will be crawling. She will begin to move around on her hands and knees anytime between the ages of six and 10 months. But don't panic if your baby is a bit hesitant about crawling! She is probably busy concentrating on some other skill, such as handling objects or making verbal sounds. In the meantime, you can do some exercises with your baby to help her prepare her arms and legs for crawling. In general, try to provide safe surroundings that encourage movement.

Holding on to one block while grasping another.

Sit on the floor with your legs stretched out in front of you. Lean your baby crosswise over your legs on her tummy, with her feet on the floor and her face turned toward you. Place a favorite toy next to you where she can see it as she peers over your thighs. As she tries to reach for the toy, she should push against the floor with her feet. (She may also wave her arms.) If she doesn't push, jiggle the toy and talk to her in order to spark her interest: **"Look at this pretty ball — it makes music when I move it. Can you get it?"**

Use several toys to help your baby do the following arm exercise. Lie on your back on the floor and place toys on both sides of you. Then lay your baby facedown on your stomach, with her head toward yours. Jiggle the toys with your hands so that she notices them. As your baby tries to reach for the toys on either side, she will push and pull herself around with her arms. As she becomes more skilled at moving herself around, she may crawl or roll off your body in order to get the toys. 🧸

9.   PULLING TO A STAND

Age Range
6-9 months

Materials
• Noisemaker

At this age your baby enjoys practicing and mastering the motor skills he is ready for. These include rolling over, sitting up, creeping, and perhaps crawling. He might also be ready to pull himself to a stand by holding on to a piece of furniture or some other support. You can spend some enjoyable moments introducing this new skill to your baby and helping him practice.

Before you begin this activity, make sure that your baby is ready for it. He should be able to stand on your lap while you hold his hands, or stand on the floor while he holds on to furniture. Place any unstable pieces of furniture out of his range. These might include pole lamps, lightweight chairs or end tables, rocking chairs, or narrow bookcases.

Place your baby on his hands and knees in front of a sofa or armchair. Put a noisemaking toy on the chair. Then make noise with the toy to get your baby's attention: **"What's that jingling sound? Stand up and see what's up here."** Place your baby's hands on the edge of the chair and lift him slowly by the waist. If he doesn't try to stand on his feet when you lift him, give him some help. Place one of his feet on the floor and lift him. He should

A baby can learn to pull to a stand even in a crib.

then put his other foot on the floor and push himself to a stand.

Help your baby practice pulling to a stand for a short time every day until he can do it alone. Praise any effort he makes: **"Look at you standing! (Baby's name) is standing."** ✖

10. STACKING BEAN BAGS

Age Range
9-12 months

Materials
- Bean bags (see *Educating on a Shoestring*)
- Assorted small plastic tubs and containers, cereal boxes, sponges, or blocks

Bean bags are easy to make and can be used in lots of ways. You can play a game of catch with them. Your baby can learn about textures if you make them with different types of fabric. Simply squishing the bag to feel the beans inside is an interesting experience. The bean bags can be dropped into containers and then poured out (as in Activity 12 of *Teaching—Family Style*). This activity uses bean bags for stacking.

If this is your baby's first experience with bean bags, give her plenty of time to get acquainted with them. Talk to her about them: **"This is a bean bag. Feel the beans inside. The outside is soft, isn't it?"** If you have several bean bags made of different types of fabric, let your baby hold and feel each one. Once she is familiar with the bean bags, you are ready to play the game.

Sit down on the floor, facing your baby. Place a bean bag between you. Slowly place another bean bag on top of it. Make sure your baby is watching you. **"Look! I stacked the bean bags."** Wait for her to pick up the bean bag on top. If she doesn't, pick it up yourself and stack them once again: **"I put the red bean bag on top of the blue bean bag. Can you stack the bean bags?"** Remove the bean bag and hand it to your baby, saying, **"You put it on top."** Point to the bean bag on the floor to show your baby where to put the one she is holding. Guide her hand if she needs help and loosen her fingers so she drops the

bean bag. **"You did it! You stacked it."**
Encourage her to stack them again.

Stacking blocks two-high.

You can play the game with other objects.
When you are in the kitchen, give your
baby empty margarine tubs or cottage
cheese containers to stack. Small cereal
boxes are also good for stacking. When
giving your baby a bath, encourage her to
stack two sponges. She can stack blocks on
the floor. After some practice, your baby
will stack two objects with ease. That's the
time to add another object so she is
stacking three-high. ✖

11.   TWO GAMES FOR TWO PEOPLE

Age Range
9-12 months

Materials
• None

Playing simple games with your baby
shows him what it means to be a partner in
play. But it won't be until about age three
that he will play in a meaningful and

cooperative way with another child. For
now he can learn that it's fun to play with
someone else, especially mommy or
daddy. Since both of the following games
are active, your baby will enjoy them most
when he is full of energy and in a playful
mood.

Most babies like to bounce up and down. It
is especially fun to bounce up and down
on a "horse" — your foot. The experience
is complete when you throw in a few
"whinnies" and "whoas." To change from
being dad or mom to being horse, simply
cross your legs. Seat your baby on your
foot so he is facing you, keeping hold of his
hands. Bounce your leg up and down very
slowly. If your baby likes this "horseback"
riding, you can speed the ride up to a
gentle gallop. As your baby rides, chant
the following rhyme:

> *Ride a cork horse,*
> *To Banbury Cross,*
> *To see a fine lady,*
> *On a white horse.*

You may find your leg tires of the game
long before your baby does.

"Row, Row, Row Your Boat" is another
simple game your baby may enjoy. Sit
down on the floor facing him. Place your
legs around him so your feet are behind his
back. Take hold of your baby's hands. Sing
"Row, row, row your boat" as you lean
forward and backward. As you lean
forward, your baby will be leaning
backward and as you lean backward, he
will be leaning forward. Start out by
moving slowly. If your baby is enjoying
the movement, you can "row" a little
faster. He may like to lean way back each
time, or he may prefer a more gentle boat
ride. ✖

12.   CRAWLING AFTER "WIGGLY"

Age Range
9-12 months

Materials
• Plastic tape measure or 1 yard of colorful yarn

Your baby may not be satisfied with simply practicing skills she has just learned. When it seems as if she has just mastered sitting up, she'll discover the tall green thing in the lovely, shiny pot and off she'll go — or try to go. Don't panic and rush to the rescue of your plant. Your baby's first attempts at crawling will probably get her nowhere. In fact, she is very likely to go backward.

Don't forget entirely about the plant, however. This is a good time to start "baby proofing" your home by removing prized possessions and hazardous objects (such as most plants) from your baby's reach. Make your home a safe place for an inquisitive, on-the-go baby. When your baby is learning to crawl, you will also want to give some thought to the way you dress her. Learning to crawl is a big enough challenge without having on clothes that make it more difficult. Feet can get caught in pants that are too long, and a long dress gets caught under little knees. Your baby can become very frustrated trying to crawl on linoleum while wearing socks — her feet may keep slipping out from behind her. The task will be a lot easier if you put a pair of sneakers on her.

You can't *teach* your baby to crawl — she must be developmentally ready. But once she starts trying to crawl, you can encourage her efforts and make the practicing fun. With a plastic tape measure or one yard of colorful yarn, you can turn the job of crawling into a game.

When you notice your baby trying to crawl, place one end of the tape measure in front of her, about 3' away. Hold the middle of the tape measure and wiggle it back and forth. Encourage your baby to reach for it: **"Get Wiggly. Come and get him."** When your baby reaches Wiggly, give her a big hug for her effort and let her play with the tape measure as she wishes. If the baby tries to get Wiggly by flopping on her belly and stretching forward, let her have the tape measure. Try the activity again though. Your baby may crawl after the tape measure the next time it is wiggled in front of her. ✖

A caterpillar puppet makes a good "Wiggly."

13. DANCING TOGETHER

Age Range
12-15 months

Materials
• Record player or radio

Whether you dance a graceful waltz or a lively polka, your baby will enjoy being held in your arms and moving around the room in rhythm to music. A good time to dance is when your baby wants your attention and is in a playful mood. All you need is your baby, some open space, and a source of music such as a radio, record player, or your own voice.

Turn the music on, pick your baby up, and ask him for the next dance! Try to make your movements fit the music. If the music is slow and smooth, a few sways, dips, and turns may be appropriate. If the music is more lively, some bouncing and twisting may be in order. To acquaint your baby with rhythm, you can sing some "la-las" to the beat of the music. You can also step to the beat of the music.

Once your baby can stand steadily on two feet, you can teach him several dance "steps." Start by clapping your hands to the beat of the music. Encourage him to clap with you. Do other simple movements for your baby to copy. You can bounce up and down, twist back and forth, and swing your arms from side to side. Get your legs moving as well. Show him how to walk in place to the beat of the music. Have him take your hands and walk a few steps forward (you'll be walking backward) and then sideways.* You may need to get on your knees to be at your baby's level. While holding hands, swing your arms from side to side, swaying with each swing of your

arms. After only a few times you may find your baby "dancing" spontaneously when he hears music playing.

Most babies love to put on dancin' shoes!

14. PLAYING A GAME OF "CHECKERS"

Age Range
12-15 months

Materials
• 6-cup muffin tin
• Objects to fit inside cups (larger than 1" diameter): spools, nontoxic blocks, or large checkers
• Large decorative magnets (optional)

In this version of "Checkers" just about anything goes and everybody is a winner. While playing the game, your baby will be coordinating eye movements with hand movements. She will also be learning to be a partner in play.

Sit on the floor with your baby and place the muffin tin between you. Put an object into three of the cups. Then take out one of the objects and place it in one of the empty cups. Encourage your baby to do the same: **"Pick up a block and put it into a cup."**

---

*By letting the baby hold *your* hands (instead of your holding *his*), he can avoid injury if he starts to fall and can't hold on. Many babies injure their shoulders or elbow joints when adults give a sudden jerk to keep them from falling.

Point to a block and then to an empty cup as you talk. Help your baby if she needs it. Continue the game as long as she is interested.

If your baby is eager, she may not pause long enough for you to get a turn. Or she may help you out by picking up an object and handing it to you. You can then promptly put it into one of the empty cups. Or your baby may make up her own rules and prefer to place two or more blocks in one cup.

You can vary the game a bit by using large decorative magnets (larger than 1" diameter). Turn the muffin tin over and place each magnet on a cup. Take turns with your baby picking up a magnet and placing it on an empty cup. ✖

15. LOOKING AT PHOTOGRAPHS OF BABY

Age Range
12-15 months

Materials
• Photographs of baby and family

If you have photographs of your baby displayed in your home, he has probably noticed them already.* He may stare with an outstetched arm, pointing at the photograph. He may even have a word or two to say to the familiar face. Photographs appeal to most babies. You can share some special moments with yours by looking through a photograph album containing pictures of him.

Sit in a comfortable chair with your baby on your lap. Say, **"We are going to look at pictures of you when you were little."** Point to each picture as you talk about it: **"This is a picture of you when you were born. You were so little. Here is a picture of Grandma holding you when you were very little. In this picture you are giving Daddy a big hug. Look, Daddy is smiling. He likes you to hug him."**

Your baby may not want to look at each picture on the page, so pick out one or two to talk about. Let him turn the pages, giving help if he needs it. Your baby isn't going to understand everything you are telling him, but he'll enjoy looking at the pictures with you. He may recognize some of the more recent pictures of himself. To help him make the connection between the picture and himself, point to your baby and say his name. Then point to the picture and say his name again. Encourage him to point to the picture and to repeat his name after you. This is all part of developing a self-concept. ✖

---

*We suggest that you label all photos with dates, names, and occasions. This makes for happy — and more complete — memories in future years.

16. PRETENDING TO TALK ON THE TELEPHONE

Age Range
15-18 months

Materials
• 2 phones (play or real)

We often drop whatever we're doing to answer a ringing telephone. Even your baby may interrupt her play to turn toward a ringing phone. She has probably watched you talk on the phone dozens of times. Since she gets a great deal of pleasure from imitating you, she'll probably enjoy pretending to talk on the phone.

Seat your baby on the floor near the phone you will be using. Place the other phone in front of her. To avoid beeps and buzzes from a real phone, unplug the phone or put a piece of masking tape over the buttons. Since your baby's vocabulary is limited, you may want to stick to the basics at first: pick up the phone when it "rings," hold it to her ear and say hi, say good-bye, and then hang up the phone.

Introduce the activity by saying, **"Let's pretend to talk on the phone. *Ring, ring.* The phone is ringing. Pick it up, (baby's name)."** Pick up your phone and hold it to your ear as an example to your baby. Say "hi" and pause to see if she will say "hi" after you. If not, encourage her by saying, **"Mommy said hi to you. Can you say hi to Mommy? Hi!"** If your baby repeats "hi" after you, try saying good-bye. Pause to see if your baby will say "bye" and then hang up the phone. If she doesn't hang up her phone, encourage her to do so: **"Hang up the phone. Put the phone down."** Guide her hand if necessary. Your baby may not be quite ready to learn telephone procedure. She may pick up the phone

Even young babies like to play with telephones.

before it rings. She may respond to your "hi" with a "hi" or a "bye" and then hang up on you. You can be an example to your baby, but always keep the telephone-talking fun even if it means bending the rules a bit.

Once your baby catches on to the basics, you may want to expand the conversation. You can try saying a word your baby knows and then pause to see if she will repeat it. If this is a success, try a few more words. Or, if your baby is a good listener, you can tell her what's for dinner, talk about the weather, or discuss anything else that might interest her. She may want to take a more active part in the conversation and may "talk" back in a language all her own. Or, if your baby is not one for many words, she may still prefer a quick "hi" followed with a "bye."

17. ENJOYING A BOOK

Age Range
15-18 months

Materials
• Picture books

Books can give even very young children hours of enjoyment and loads of information. If your baby develops an interest in books while he is young, it may continue into later years. Give your baby an opportunity to develop that interest by regularly looking at and reading picture books with him. He'll enjoy listening to a story while naming and commenting on people, actions, and objects pictured in the book.

Select books with simple stories and colorful pictures. Books with pictures of things your baby is familiar with, such as toys, animals, and people, are especially good. See *Educating on a Shoestring* for ideas for books you can make. A good time to look at a book with your baby is when he is winding down before a nap or bedtime, or when he just wants your attention and wants to be held.

If the book has a simple story, you may want to read it to your baby. If the story is too advanced, talk about the pictures. Name the objects in the pictures, talk about what the characters are doing, and point out colors. You can also amuse your baby with sound effects by "mooing" for the cow and "choo-chooing" for the train. Your baby may also enjoy turning the pages. Encourage him to turn them by himself. But if he needs some help, lift the corner of the page for him.

Some books will appeal more than others to your baby. He may never seem to tire of looking at the pictures in certain books or hearing the stories. Over time he will begin to put names and pictures together. When this happens, ask him to point to things in the pictures: **"Point to the worm. Where's the worm?"** Once he is pointing at the things you name, ask him to name things you point to: **"What's that?"** Wait several seconds and then name what you are pointing to: **"It is a car."** Ask your baby again what it is. He may not hesitate to tell you! ✳

18. SOLVING SIMPLE PROBLEMS

Age Range
15-18 months

Materials
• 2 washcloths or plastic cups of different colors
• Small object to fit under cloth or cup (larger than 1" diameter)

Have you ever watched a magician place an object under one of three cups and then shuffle the cups around? The object is never under the cup you think it's under! This activity is a simple version of that trick. Of course, you aren't trying to trick your baby, although at times she might think that's exactly what you've done. Rather you will be giving her a chance to solve simple problems.

Sit opposite your baby on the floor. Show her the object and let her play with it. Place one of the washcloths on the floor. Once she will let you, take the object away from your baby and place it under the cloth. She will probably pick the cloth up immediately to discover the toy, which she already knew was there. Then hold the toy in your hand and close your hand. Put the toy under the cloth and remove your hand, keeping it closed. If your baby doesn't open your hand, show her the toy is no longer there. If she doesn't look under the cloth for the toy, point to the cloth and ask her to look under it: **"Look under the cloth. The toy is there. Good, you found it."**

The game becomes even more challenging when you add a second cloth. Let your baby see the toy in your hand. Hide the toy under one of the cloths and then show her that it is no longer in your hand. Wait to **see if she will look under the correct cloth.**

A not-so-simple problem: finding a block hidden under one of three cups.

You can play one other version of the game by placing the toy under one of the cloths. Then, while your baby is watching, remove it and place it under the other cloth. Tell her what you are doing as you place the object under the second cloth: **"Now I am hiding the car under the red cloth. Where is the car?"** There is a good chance your baby will pick up the cloth that you put the object under first. If so, help her discover which cloth the toy is actually under. Point to the cloth: **"Look under the red cloth. The toy is hiding under there."** ⭐

Just for the Fun of It

1. Watching Movement
2. Looking in a Mirror Alone
3. Listening
4. Kicking a Toy
5. Looking in a Mirror Together
6. Looking at What I'm Holding
7. Enjoying My Reflection in a Mirror
8. Moving to Music
9. Pouring from a Container
10. Playing "Catch Me"
11. Playing with Paper
12. Touring the House
13. Riding on a Towel
14. Feats with Feet
15. Touch the Light
16. Playing in a Sandbox
17. Pulling a String to Get a Toy
18. Finger-Painting

1.   WATCHING MOVEMENT

Age Range
Birth-3 months

Materials
• Flashlight, watch, pendant, or piece of foil

Your baby's ability to coordinate his* eye movements and follow moving objects will improve greatly during the first three months. Newborns can best see things that are at least 8" away, but they stare only momentarily at objects in their view. During the first month they begin to look more carefully at things, but they won't turn to look at something as it disappears from their sight. During the second month they begin to follow moving objects with their eyes, and by the third month they'll turn their head to watch something as it moves.

Use a small flashlight or shiny object to play a looking game with your baby. This game will change over the first three months as your infant's ability to track an object improves. Play for very brief periods of time in order to hold your baby's attention.

Hold the light or attractive object in front of your baby's face, at least 8" away. Do not shine the light into the baby's eyes. Move it back and forth. If he follows the movement with his eyes, move it up and down. When he can follow an object moving up and down, move it in circles.

As soon as your baby can follow objects with his eyes, see if he will turn his head to watch them as they move out of sight. First move the flashlight or object to one side so that the baby can no longer see it. If he doesn't turn to look, talk from where the

The darting of a goldfish can fascinate an infant.

object now is to attract his attention: **"Here it is, (baby's name). Look at the bright light. It moved!"** Bring it back in front of his face. Then move it up over his head and out of sight. Talk to him from the new position so that he looks in that direction. Bring it back in front of him and down toward his toes. By the end of the third month, he might reach for the object as he watches it. Let him touch the object as you talk about how it feels: **"This shiny flashlight is smooth. It feels warm from the bulb."**

2.   LOOKING IN A MIRROR ALONE

Age Range
Birth-3 months

Materials
• Large mirror

Your baby is beginning to learn about the world she* sees by studying everything in view. Brightly colored and moving objects especially catch her eye. If you have a large mirror, your infant will enjoy watching her own image as she waves and wiggles.

---

*In odd-numbered activities, the baby is referred to as a boy. In even-numbered activities, the baby is referred to as a girl.

---

*In even-numbered activities, the baby is referred to as a girl. In odd-numbered activities, the baby is referred to as a boy.

Use a mirror that is at least the size of your baby. Lean the mirror against the wall on the floor or next to the crib. Be sure to secure the mirror to the wall so that it doesn't fall over or slide down onto the floor. Arrange a comfortable area next to the mirror for the baby to lie on. For example, you might place a soft blanket on the floor. Of course, never leave your baby alone on an elevated surface. Even though she seems unable to move around at this age, a sudden kick or body movement could send her toppling onto the floor. To make her image more attractive to her, dress your baby in a bright color or lively print, or tie a red or orange ribbon around her wrist.

Place your baby next to the mirror, close enough so that she can touch it. If she doesn't look toward the mirror, turn her head in that direction. She will soon be attracted to her own face and active body. Enjoy watching your baby play, but don't distract her with your voice. Let her enjoy herself! ✸

3. LISTENING

Age Range
Birth-3 months

Materials
• Nontoxic rattle, bell, or set of metal measuring spoons

By the second month your baby will listen closely to noises that he hears. Most infants are fascinated with sounds and especially enjoy toys that have music boxes or other noisemakers inside. You can play a simple sound game with your little one by using a rattle, a bell, or a set of metal measuring spoons.

Lay the baby in his bed or on a blanket on the floor. Stand behind his head so that he can't see you. Hold the noisemaker above your baby's forehead, slightly out of his sight. Shake the toy quietly and slowly so you don't startle him. He should look up to see the noisy object.* When he looks, smile at him and talk about the sound: **"That was a surprise, wasn't it? A bell made that sound."** Then hold the noisemaker to one side of the baby's head and shake it faster. If he still looks in your direction rather than toward the sound, move out of his sight while you shake the toy.

If you don't have a rattle handy, try your voice!

If the baby enjoys the game, use a different noisemaker and repeat the activity. Play this sound game for no more than five minutes or you will overstimulate your infant and tire him out. ✸

---

*If you see that your baby is not responding to the sound, be sure to have his hearing checked.

4.   KICKING A TOY

Age Range
3-6 months

Materials
- Piece of string 12" long
- Noisemaker: bell, plastic container or tightly-capped bottle containing dried beans, or rattle

Every day, your baby is discovering new actions she can perform with her body. She can twist and turn to see things out of view. She can hold things and bring them to her mouth in order to taste and explore them. With the following simple game you can introduce your baby to her feet and inspire her to use them for kicking things.

Attach a lightweight noisemaker to a string (about 12" long). Then lay your baby on her back and remove her booties or socks if she's wearing any.

Hold the toy by the string and jiggle it up and down above the baby's feet. Say: **"Look at this. You can kick it with your feet."** Your baby may wave her feet and arms in excitement. Let the toy rest on a foot. She will probably kick in reaction. If not, tap her foot with the toy until she kicks back. Once your baby discovers that she can make the toy move and produce sound when she kicks it, she'll continue to kick! Talk to her as she kicks, and enjoy the game with her.

After you finish the game, hang the noise-making toy over your baby's feet in her playpen or crib. This way she can play the kicking game when she is alone. Be sure to tie the string securely to the pen or crib so that the baby can't get tangled in the string. 🧩

5.   LOOKING IN A MIRROR
         TOGETHER

Age Range
3-6 months

Materials
- Large mirror

You and your baby can spend some enjoyable moments looking into a mirror. Use a wall mirror or a large mirror securely propped against a wall so that you can both look at your reflections.

Hold your baby upright and look into the mirror cheek to cheek. Position yourselves fairly close to your reflections and talk to your baby: **"Who's that? Is it you with your cute bald head? Is it me with my big curly head?"** Your baby may be puzzled to see you *in front of* him in the mirror and yet **hear** your voice *next to* him. Make silly

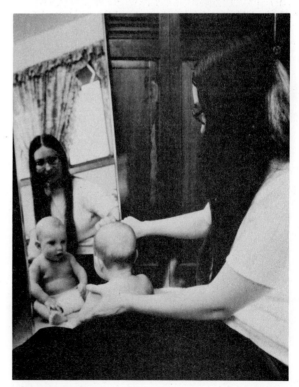

Looking in a mirror.

faces and noises, and kiss your baby as you play.

Rock your baby toward the mirror and away again as you say in a singsong voice:

> *Rocking, rocking,*
> *Back and forth we're rocking.*
> *Back and forth, back and forth,*
> *(Baby's name) and (Daddy/Mommy) are*
> *rocking.*

As you rock forward, let your baby's forehead lightly touch the mirror. Afterward, hold his hand on the mirror and let him feel his reflection. 🧍

At another time, when she is *not* looking at her hands, put the toy in one of your baby's hands. See if she brings the toy to her face and looks at it. If not, raise her hand to her face for her and talk about the toy that she's holding: **"Here's your toy mouse. He wants to see you."** Try this game with other toys at different times. Eventually your baby will quickly bring the toy to her face to see what she is holding. 🧍

6.   LOOKING AT WHAT I'M HOLDING

Age Range
3-6 months

Materials
• Brightly colored plaything small enough to fit in baby's hand (larger than 1" diameter): rattle, squeeze toy, teething ring, or Ping-Pong ball

By this time your baby is very interested in her hands. She will spend a great deal of time watching them move, tasting them, and trying to use them for grasping and holding objects. You can play a quick game with your baby by using a small toy that she can hold.

While your baby is busy looking at her hands, put a small toy in one of them. She'll be delighted to see the toy appear in her hand. Talk to her about it: **"Look at the funny mouse. He's wearing a green coat!"** During the fourth month, your baby will still let go of the object after a short while. But by the sixth month, she will be able to hold on to and let go of the toy as she wishes. Allow your baby to examine the toy as long as she wants.

7. ENJOYING MY REFLECTION IN A MIRROR

Age Range
6-9 months

Materials
• Large mirror
• Towel

Your baby probably breaks into a grin whenever he sees himself in a mirror. You can help him learn more about himself and about language while he stares at his reflection. To play the following game, use a mirror in which your baby can easily see his reflection.

While you and your baby look in the mirror, point to him and say his name: **"You're (Jason). Jason."** Then point to yourself and say your own name. **"I'm (Grandma)."** Repeat each name several times in a playful way while you look at yourselves: **"I'm going to tickle Jason. Now I'll tickle Grandma."**

Play peek-a-boo using the mirror and a towel. Hold the towel in front of the mirror and ask, **"Where are you? Where's Jason?"** Then pull the towel away and make sure that your baby looks at his reflection:

Who's that baby?

"There's Jason. Peek-a-boo! And there's Grandma, too."

Point to two or three body parts on your baby and name them: **"Here's your nose."** You might tap his nose playfully as you repeat the label: **"Nose. Nose. Nose."** If you repeat the game and name the body parts often, your baby will eventually understand that word. ✿

8. MOVING TO MUSIC

Age Range
6-9 months

Materials
• Record player or radio

When your baby hears music she may become excited and wave her arms, kick her legs, or make sounds as if she were trying to sing. On the other hand, she may not respond in any way that you can see. She may listen and enjoy the music in her own quiet way. You and your baby can enjoy moving to music together as you sing or listen to a recording.

Sit down and seat your baby on your lap, facing you. If you enjoy singing to your baby, try the following song to the tune of "A Hunting We Will Go." Do the accompanying motions with your baby while you sing:

> *A-clapping we will go,*
> (Clap baby's hands together)
> *A-clapping we will go,*
> *Hi, ho the dairy-o,*
> *A-clapping we will go.*

Some extra verses:

> *A-bouncing we will go . . .*
> (Bounce baby up and down while she sits)

A-twisting we will go . . .
(Twist baby's body from side to side)

A-dancing we will go . . .
(Hold baby with your hands around
her rib cage; pull her to a stand and
bounce her up and down)

Play recorded music as you move your
baby to the rhythm of the tune. Repeat the
motions above and try some new ones.
You might rock her to and fro, lay her on
her back and clap the soles of her feet
together, dance around the room while
you hold her, or turn around in circles
while you rock her to the beat. ✳

To dump comes first — to aim comes later!

9. POURING FROM A CONTAINER

Age Range
6-9 months

Materials
- Objects (larger than 1" diameter) to fit
  in containers: spools or blocks
- Containers: plastic measuring cups or
  food-storage tubs

Your baby is discovering that he can make
things happen. When he pushes
something with his hand, it moves. When
he shakes a rattle, it makes noise. When
he crushes a cracker in his fist, it changes
shape. And when he plays with a
container filled with objects, all sorts of
things happen! He can learn how to empty
it.

Put some objects into a plastic measuring
cup or a small food-storage container.
Show the container to your baby and tip it
over so that the objects pour out onto the
floor: **"Look at what came out of the
measuring cup! You can do it, too."**

Put the objects back into the container.
Then hand it to your baby. He may decide
to explore the container and taste the
things that are in it. Let him play freely
with the objects for a while. Then take his
hand and help him empty the contents of
the container onto the floor. Put the things
back into the container and help him
empty it again: **"You did it! The blocks are
on the floor."**

Eventually your baby may try to empty the
container by himself. When he does, praise
him and give him a big hug. ✳

10. PLAYING "CATCH ME"

Age Range
9-12 months

Materials
• None

The first time your baby crawls is a joyous moment. But several months may pass between the time she crawls those first few yards and the time she ventures freely throughout the house. When your baby first learns to crawl she will probably be content to explore the room you put her in. Being able to get around on her own opens up all kinds of possibilities, but none of them rivals her desire to be near you. A problem may arise, however, when *you* decide to leave *her*. Your baby may watch you walk down the hallway and turn into the bedroom. But since she is not used to being able to follow you, she may not even try. A hallway can look like a long, lonesome road. To bring you back to her side she may use a tried and true method — a loud wail.

To help your baby get used to following you from room to room, you can play a game of "Catch Me." Begin the game in your living room. Get down on all fours

Playing a game of "Catch Dad."

and crawl away from your baby. Then look back at her and say, **"Come and get me, (baby's name)."** When your baby reaches you, laugh and cuddle her: **"Good for you. You caught me."** Put your baby down and crawl away from her again. She may crawl after you or she may wait until you stop, turn around, and invite her to catch up with you.

If your baby waits for an invitation to follow you, the activity can be turned into a game of hide and seek. Crawl about 8' and then encourage your baby to come after you. When she does, give her a hug. Then crawl again for about 8'. When you come to a room, dodge inside the doorway. Peek out of the doorway at your baby and encourage her to come after you: **"Here I am. Come and get me."** Then move so she can't see you. If she crawls a few feet and stops before reaching you, pop your head out to remind her where you are. When she reaches you, say, **"Peek-a-boo. You caught me."** You may want to crawl to another hiding place in the room and into the doorway of another room. Pop your head out of the doorway so your baby can see where you have gone. Continue the game as long as she is enjoying it.

11. PLAYING WITH PAPER

Age Range
9-12 months

Materials
• Paper: wax paper, aluminum foil, fine-grade sandpaper, tissue paper, paper towel, construction paper
• Box, bag, or bowl

You may have discovered by now that store-bought toys are not always the answer to keeping your baby busy. Many toys are designed to promote your baby's development, and he may enjoy playing with them. But you may also have watched your baby have just as much fun batting at an empty toilet-paper roll and watching it roll across the floor, or pushing an empty milk carton around the room. Babies don't know — and don't care — whether a plaything costs a lot of money.

When your baby seems to be looking for something different to do, try giving him various kinds of paper to examine, crinkle, and tear. Place the paper in a box, bag, or bowl and set it in front of him. Each type of paper will, of course, look different. Each will also sound different to your baby as he crushes it in his hands. Your baby will discover that some paper feels soft and some feels rough, and that some tears easily and some is very difficult to tear. Be careful to keep the paper out of the baby's mouth. Many colored wrapping papers contain lead dyes, which are poisonous.

During many activities it is helpful to talk to your baby about what he's doing and about the objects he's exploring. That's true for this activity, too. But you may also enjoy just sitting back in an easy chair and watching your baby — if he'll let you. He may explore the paper vigorously or cautiously. He may tear each piece into tiny bits or give each piece a toss. Or he may take each piece out of the container and then very purposefully put each piece back in. Watching him struggle with a piece of sticky tape can be a show in itself.

12. TOURING THE HOUSE

Age Range
9-12 months

Materials
- None

Your baby is probably an expert at exploring the things in your house that are less than 2 1/2' off the floor. To see things higher than that she depends on you, or someone else, for a boost up. She has probably caught glimpses of pictures, clocks, and bookshelves as you've carried her through the house to be diapered, dressed, and fed. Some very interesting things have undoubtedly caught her eye which she would love to examine more closely. You can give your baby this opportunity by taking her on a slow tour of your house.

Pick several rooms in your house to include in the tour. Other rooms can be toured on other days. Carry your baby through the room, stopping at various points of interest. Talk about each thing you look at. Let your baby explore it in whatever way is appropriate. She may listen to it, touch it, smell it, taste it, or watch a demonstration of how it works. She'll enjoy looking at pictures, especially if they are of people she is familiar with. Watching you flick a light switch on and off is a fascinating experience. Take your baby's finger and help her flick it on and off several times. Lights with dimmer switches are especially interesting. Door knobs feel cool and are fun to turn. Your baby will get a real treat if you have a wall clock with a pendulum that sways back and forth. If you have a piano, let her watch as you play a note or two. Or let her feel the cold air on her face as you open the freezer door.

The things your baby experiences on her tour will be as unique as your home. She will enjoy the things you show her and will especially enjoy your company as you share your time and yourself with her.

13.   RIDING ON A TOWEL

Age Range
12-15 months

Materials
• Beach towel, crib-size blanket, or quilt

If your baby likes movement, he may enjoy a ride through the house on a towel. But don't try this activity until your baby is sitting up and can maintain his balance well. If he is balancing well while sitting, this activity will give him some practice balancing while moving — something he'll have to do when he starts walking.

Lay a beach towel or a crib-size blanket or quilt on the floor (linoleum or wooden floors work best). You will move slowly with your baby so he won't topple over, but for extra protection place a pillow at one end of the towel. This way he won't hurt himself if he falls backward.

Seat your baby in the middle of the towel with the pillow behind him. Gather up the other end of the towel in your hands and face him. Begin to move backward very slowly: **"I'm taking you for a ride. Here we go. We will go very slowly. Isn't this fun?"** If the expression on your baby's face shows that he's not so sure this is fun, stop

the activity. But if his face lights up with a smile, take him for a ride through the house. If he is keeping his balance well, walk a little faster. ✳

A harder feat: riding on a scooter, instead of a towel.

14.   FEATS WITH FEET

Age Range
12-15 months

Materials
• Dishpan
• Rice, salt, sand, or cream of wheat
• Paper, plastic, or tile
• Carpet sample
• Fur, feather, or cotton ball

Your baby's hands are probably very busy these days. She is surrounded by a lot of very interesting things, and she may not be satisfied until she has examined each one. But what about her feet? Have they been getting their fair share of life's experiences? If not, these next activities will be new and entertaining.

Give your baby's feet the sensation of feeling something bumpy by placing some rice in a dishpan. If you have a child-size chair or a jump seat, place your baby in it and slide the dishpan under her bare feet. If her feet don't touch the rice, place some catalogs or magazines under the dishpan until they do. Take hold of your baby's ankles and slowly move her feet around in the rice. Talk about what you are doing and how it feels: **"I am moving your feet around in the rice. It feels bumpy, doesn't it?"** For a different experience, put salt, sand, or a fine cereal such as uncooked cream of wheat in the dishpan.

While your baby is sitting she may also enjoy rubbing her feet across something smooth and slick. A carpet sample under her feet can feel rough and bumpy. A piece of fur, a feather, or a cotton ball feels soft and may tickle. If your baby is walking, talk about how it feels as she walks barefoot on tile, carpet, wood, cement, and through grass and leaves: **"The grass is soft and it tickles. The cement feels rough and it's hard."** It will be a while before your baby understands the meaning of these words, but she will have fun as she's introduced to the various textures. ✗

15.   TOUCH THE LIGHT

Age Range
12-15 months

Materials
• Flashlight

Since he was very young, moving objects have caught your baby's eye. A mobile swaying in the breeze or the movement of the picture on the TV set has probably captured and kept his attention many times. This activity uses a moving light to attract your baby's attention. You will need a darkened room and a light colored wall. Move any furniture or objects so that you have at least 6' of empty space on the wall.

In the darkened room, seat your baby a couple of feet in front of the wall so that he is facing it. Sit next to him and explain that you are going to play a game with light. Ask him to look at the wall. Turn on the flashlight and shine the light on the wall in front of your baby: **"Look! There's a light. Can you touch the light?"** If he doesn't seem to understand, take his hand and help him touch the light. **"You're touching the light."** Turn the flashlight off. **"Where did the lights go?"** Turn the flashlight on again. **"There it is. Can you touch it?"**

Turn the flashlight off again and ask your baby where the light is as you move behind him. When you turn it on, aim it at a spot on the wall which your baby can touch only by getting up and reaching. **"Where's the light? It is way over there. Can you go get it? Touch the light."** If your baby doesn't seem to understand, demonstrate by touching the light yourself. Try to keep the light in the same spot as you move. **"I'm touching the light. Can you touch it?"**

Continue playing the game as long as your baby is interested. Shine the light on different spots on the wall and ask him to touch the light. The first time or two that you play, your baby may be more interested in the flashlight than the game. If so, let him hold the flashlight. Show him how to turn it on and off. Once his curiosity is satisfied, he may be ready to play the game. If not, you can try it again some other day. ✗

16. PLAYING IN A SANDBOX

Age Range
15-18 months

Materials
- Sandbox
- Toys and tools: cars, trucks, plastic cups, spoons, scoops, muffin tins, bowls
- Cereal, plastic baby bath, and old sheet (optional)

You don't have to watch children playing in a sandbox or at the beach very long to see how much fun sand can be. With a little direction from you, your baby can enjoy learning some important skills such as scooping, pouring, and stirring. Your baby can also practice these skills in the bathtub, since water and sand have similar characteristics. But sand feels different from water, and so it provides a different experience.

Scooping indoors — not as messy, but just as fun.

If you don't have access to a sandbox, sand play can be turned into "cereal play." You can't build with cereal as you can with sand. But it is cleaner, which is an advantage if your baby is still testing things out by putting them into her mouth. (Corn meal and cream of wheat both work well for "cereal play." Oatmeal isn't as suitable because it can stick to the roof of your baby's mouth and cause her to choke.) You will also need a tub in which to put the cereal. A plastic baby bath works well because your baby can sit in it as she plays. She can also sit next to a plastic dishpan. If you are playing inside, spread a sheet out on the floor and put the cereal box in the middle of it. Cereal on the floor can be slippery and dangerous. The sheet also makes cleaning up easier and allows you to recover some of the cereal for future use at playtime.

First, introduce your baby to the sand* (or cereal): **"This is sand. Feel it with your hand."** Give your baby some time to explore the sand in her own way. She may pat it, poke one finger in it, or go straight into action picking up handfuls and letting it fall through her fingers. When your baby is well acquainted with the sand and seems ready for a new experience, give her an object or a pair of objects to play with. If you give your baby only one object or a set of objects at a time, you can prolong her interest.

Next, give your baby the scoop and a bowl. Show her how to scoop up the sand and pour it into the bowl. Encourage her to scoop and pour until it is full. You can remove the scoop and replace it with a spoon. Show your baby how to use the spoon to stir a bowl half full of sand. Give her a bowl and cup. Show her how to

---

*If you use sand, be sure it is the "sterilized" kind in which organic material has been treated by heat to reduce the risk of infectious disease. Uncovered sandboxes are commonly used as toilets by cats, so cover the box with a screen when it is not in use. Rain and sun can help cleanse the sand.

53

scoop sand into the cup and pour it into the bowl. She may enjoy filling the bowl by scooping the sand up with her hands. You can also wet the sand and let your baby squeeze it. Encourage her to help you pat the sand into various shapes. ✶

17. PULLING A STRING TO GET A TOY

Age Range
15-18 months

Materials
- Shoe box or tissue box with both ends cut out
- Tissue or cloth
- 15" string
- Toys to fit inside box (larger than 1" diameter)
- Tape

Solving problems is something your baby must learn to do. Fortunately your baby will view many of the problems he faces as *challenges.* A clever parent can turn problem solving into a game.

Seat your baby at a table. Tie one end of the string around a toy. Place the free end of the string in front of your baby and stretch the string out so the toy is beyond his reach. **"There's your favorite red truck.** *Honk, honk! Vroom!* **Can you get the truck?"** Give your baby some time to figure out that in order to get the truck he must pull the string. If he doesn't seem to know what to do, show him how to pull on the string. Give him plenty of time to examine and play with the "prize" on the end of the string. Try the activity one more time, using a different toy.

Once your baby has learned the pull-the-string-and-get-the-toy trick, you can make the game more fun by adding the shoe-box tunnel. Tape the tissue or cloth over one end of the box. Try to keep the toy out of your baby's sight as you tie the string around it and place it in the tunnel. Place the tunnel so the end covered with the cloth is facing your baby. Build up suspense as you talk to your baby: **"What could be in the tunnel? Pull the string and see what's in there. Here it comes. Look! It's a pig.** *Oink, oink.*"

You can play another version of this game with your baby while he is sitting in his highchair. Tie the string around a toy. Put the other end of the string in your baby's hand. Drop the toy over the side of the highchair. Ask your baby to pull the toy up. If necessary, show him how. ✶

18. FINGER-PAINTING

Age Range
15-18 months

Materials
- Nontoxic finger paint (see *Educating on a Shoestring*)
- Paper, tape
- Old clothes

Every parent's refrigerator needs at least one piece of baby's artwork displayed on the door. Grandmas and Grandpas also welcome pictures from their favorite artist — their grandchild. Your baby's first introduction to finger-painting will be a memorable one. To assure they are fond memories, take time to prepare for the event. Don't be discouraged if after all of your careful preparation, your baby doesn't spend a lot of time at the activity. This experience will be quite a new one for her, and so it may take a while for her to get the hang of it. As she gets more experience and grows older she will spend more time at her creative adventures, and she will find it a lot of fun and very satisfying.

It is important to use nontoxic paint since your baby may want to discover how it tastes as well as how it feels. See *Educating on a Shoestring* for a recipe for a flour- and a starch-base paint. Your baby can also paint with and safely taste ketchup, mustard, or chocolate pudding.

Finger-painting on a tabletop.

Seat your baby at a table that will not be harmed by paint. Glossy paper works best for finger-painting, but any kind of plain paper can be used. Tape the corners of the paper to the table. If you don't have any paper on hand, your baby can finger-paint directly on the table or on her highchair tray. She will enjoy finger-painting on a table as much as on paper, but you won't be able to enjoy her artwork in the future. Since finger-painting is messy, dress your baby in old clothes. Bibs and smocks protect her clothes some, but they also can get in the way, especially if she is an enthusiastic painter.

Seat your baby in front of the colorful goo! Guide her hand so it touches the finger paint. Let her poke at it and squeeze it between her fingers: **"It feels cool and smooth."** Help her move her hands in circles — first one hand, then the other, and finally both hands together. Show your baby how to move her fingers in small circles and big circles. Go on to have her move her hands and arms in big and in small circles as well. Once your baby is familiar with the feeling of the paint, she will experiment and create with it in her own way.

Changing Time

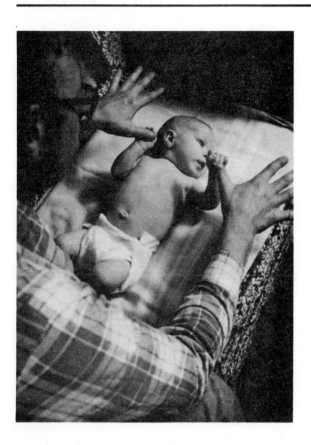

1. Taking a Look
2. Holding On
3. Touching
4. Going Up!
5. Imitating Sounds
6. Playing Peek-a-Boo
7. Tearing Paper
8. Gesturing
9. Learning Hand Movements for a Song
10. Leg and Foot Massage
11. Covering and Uncovering My Eyes
12. Changing-Time Rhymes
13. Hanging Up My Clothes
14. Helping at Dressing Time
15. Discovering a Face
16. Understanding Simple Opposites
17. Brushing Hair

1. TAKING A LOOK

   Age Range
   Birth-3 months

   Materials
   • Magazine pictures, greeting cards,
     interesting "junk" mail
   • Pegboard (optional)
   • Tape

Your baby learns much about his* world by
studying what he sees. He likes to look at
pictures that are shiny and colorful. He
would rather look at three-dimensional
objects, but a colorful picture or design can
easily grab his attention.

Since you and your baby spend a lot of
time changing diapers, take time to
arrange his changing area so that it has
interesting things to look at. You can hang
a pegboard next to the changing table at
the baby's eye level, or clear a space on the
wall next to his table. Then tape one
picture to the area you've prepared.

While you change the baby's diaper, turn
his head toward the picture. If he doesn't
notice it at first, tap the picture until he
sees it. Every morning, change the picture
and eventually hang more than one picture
at a time. When your baby is about 10
weeks old, he will begin to reach out for
the attractive picture.

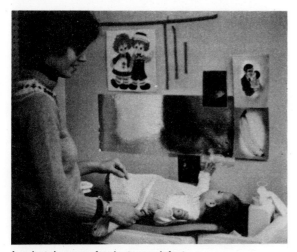

A mylar mirror may fascinate your infant.

*In odd-numbered activities, the baby is referred to as a
boy. In even-numbered activities, the baby is referred to as
a girl.

2. HOLDING ON

   Age Range
   Birth-3 months

   Materials
   • Rattle or other graspable object (larger
     than 1" diameter)

Sometime during your infant's second
month, she* will begin to reach out toward

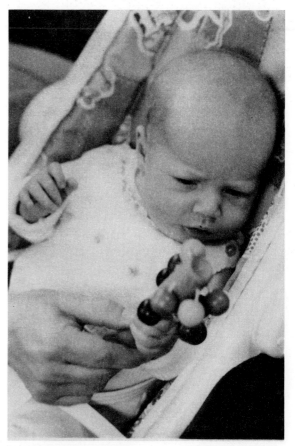

Learning to grasp a rattle.

*In even-numbered activities, the baby is referred to as a
girl. In odd-numbered activities, the baby is referred to as a
boy.

and react with her surroundings. Once she begins to bat at objects with her fist, you can help her practice holding small objects.

Keep a rattle at the baby's diaper-changing area. Then, when you're changing her, show her the rattle and shake it. If she is very interested, she'll reach toward the toy with her fist. Since she is not yet ready to grab things on her own, wrap her fingers around the rattle. She will probably drop it after a few seconds. Put the rattle back in her hand and talk to her: **"You dropped your rattle. Here it is. Now hold on tight!"**

After your baby drops it a few times, put the rattle in her other hand. During the next few weeks occasionally help her grasp the rattle. She will begin to hold it for longer and longer periods of time. 🧍

foot? Does it tickle?" Then rub the baby's palm on the material. If he enjoyed feeling the cloth, rub him with something else that is within your reach. You might use a lotion bottle, a stuffed animal, a cloth with a different texture, or a cotton ball.

At another changing time, gently rub your baby again with the same or different materials. Rub him with only one or two materials at each changing time; otherwise you might stimulate him too much and have a screaming infant who needs to be calmed. If the object you use is small and lightweight, wrap the baby's fist around it so that he can hold it. He will probably let go after a few seconds. 🧍

3.   TOUCHING

   Age Range
   Birth-3 months

   Materials
   • Clean diaper, towel, or other cloth

Everything is new to your baby, and he uses all of his senses to learn about the world, even while you're changing his diaper. Try the following suggestions to interest him in his sense of touch.

After you've changed the baby's diaper (and he is happy and comfortable), rub his arm gently with a clean diaper or some other type of cloth that is close at hand. (Do not leave your baby alone on a changing table while you look for something.) Talk to him about how the fabric feels: **"This towel is a little bit rough. I'm rubbing it lightly on your arm. Do you feel it?"** Rub the cloth on his face, his leg, and the bottom of his foot while you talk to him: **"How does it feel on your**

4. GOING UP!

Age Range
3-6 months

Materials
• None

Your baby's body is becoming stronger and more coordinated every day. If she holds her head up steadily when you place her on her belly, she may be ready to do the following pull-up exercise at changing time.

After your baby is in a clean diaper, keep her on the changing table, lying on her back. Wrap her fingers around your thumbs and talk to her: **"Hello, sweetheart. Do you want to come up?"** Then pull her slowly up with her arms extended toward you. Pull her up only an inch or two. She should hold her head

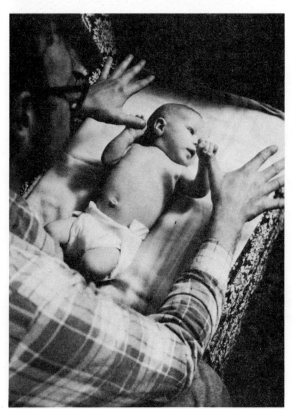

Holding on to dad's thumbs.

steady as you pull. But if her head hangs back limply, gently lower her onto the table and try this exercise again when she has more head control.

If your baby controlled her head well, pull her up an inch or two and then gently lower her again: **"You went up and down. Was that fun? You're such a strong baby!"** Repeat this exercise at least once a day. Eventually you will be able to pull her to a sitting position while she maintains good control of her head and grip. This exercise will help your baby become stronger in her hands, arms, and neck. 🧍

5. IMITATING SOUNDS

Age Range
3-6 months

Materials
• None

Talk to your baby as much as you can! Although he won't understand your words for many months, he is already using his voice to communicate feelings and to try to imitate your speech. *Anytime* is an occasion for you to talk to your baby. But while you are changing his diaper and you're both relaxed, you have a good opportunity for a short chat.

While your baby is lying on the changing table, get his attention so that he looks at your face. Then say a short sentence or phrase such as, **"Hello, little sweetheart."** If he doesn't make any sounds in response to you, talk a little more and make unusual sounds. Despite these, he may answer you with only a grin or a stare. Once he does respond with a sound or lip movement, imitate *him*. Repeat any of his gurgles, coos, lip smackings, or other baby noises. If he answers you back again, continue imitating him until you have a lively "conversation" going.

Then say a simple sound to your baby, such as "goo-goo" or "ba-ba." Repeat the same sound several times and see if he will imitate you. Praise him for any attempt he makes at the sound: **"That was almost the same thing I said. Good try!"** Over the next few days, repeat the sound for him so that he becomes very familiar with it. Even if he doesn't repeat the sound, he will begin to recognize it and enjoy it even more. ✻

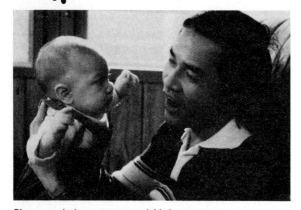
Show your baby you can speak his language.

6. PLAYING PEEK-A-BOO

Age Range
3-6 months

Materials
• Diaper, small toy

Peek-a-boo is an all-time favorite game that your baby can enjoy even at this young age. She won't understand that you are hiding behind something. To her, you have completely disappeared, and so she will be amazed and delighted when you suddenly return with a big smile.

Talk to your baby and laugh with her as you change her diaper: **"Look at me, (baby's name). I can see your pretty face."** Then while she is still on the changing table, continue to talk to her as you grab a clean diaper. Hold the diaper in front of your face briefly and then pull it away as you say, **"Peek-a-boo!"** or **"Here I am!"** Quickly hide your face again and repeat the procedure several times. Your baby might stare in amazement or grin with surprise as you disappear and come back again. When you repeat the game over the next few weeks, her response will probably change as she becomes familiar with peek-a-boo. She may wave her arms and giggle in anticipation as you hide and reappear.

Use a small toy for another version of peek-a-boo at changing time. Show the baby the plaything after you've changed her diaper. Then while she is watching the toy, hold the palm of your other hand in front of it and act surprised: **"Where is it? Where did the toy go?"** Quickly make the toy reappear and act delighted: **"Here it is! I thought it was gone."** Make the toy disappear and reappear several times. Then hand it to your baby so that she can play with it for a while. ✻

Peek-a-boo by any other name would be as fun.

7.   TEARING PAPER

Age Range
6-9 months

Materials
• "Junk" mail

By now your baby is probably wiggly and impatient when you change his diaper. But if you keep some paper handy, he can entertain himself while you change him.

Keep a supply of junk mail near your baby's changing table. Include envelopes and colorful ads, but avoid newspaper since the ink rubs off easily and makes a mess. When you change your baby, hand him a piece of paper to tear and crumple and taste.

Talk to your baby while he plays with the paper: **"You're so strong! You ripped that paper to shreds."** By the time he has demolished the paper, he will be in a clean diaper and ready to go. 🧍

8.   GESTURING

Age Range
6-9 months

Materials
• None

Gestures are a simple way to communicate ideas to your baby. After you change her diaper, you can teach her a gesture that means "I will pick you up now."

When your baby is lying on her changing table in a clean diaper, extend your arms toward her and say, **"Up!"** Then lift your baby off the table. Everytime you change her diaper, repeat the "up" gesture with her. Eventually she'll understand what the gesture means.

Next, teach your baby how to use the gesture herself to mean "Pick me up." After you extend your arms and say, "Up," hold her arms toward you. Then say, **"Of course I'll pick you up,"** and lift her off the table. After you practice many times, your baby may hold her arms toward you on her own to mean "Please pick me up." 🧍

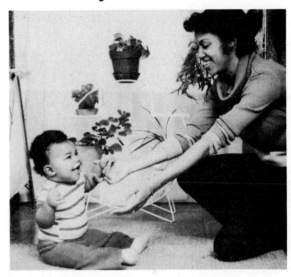
Your baby will learn to imitate your gestures.

9.   LEARNING HAND MOVEMENTS
     FOR A SONG

Age Range
6-9 months

Materials
• None

Your baby probably enjoys listening to songs and rhymes that you perform for him. And with your help, he can do some accompanying hand movements.

After you put your baby in a clean diaper, keep him on his changing table for a while. Sing the following song to the tune of

"Row, Row, Row Your Boat" while you help him do the motions:

> *Clap, clap, clap your hands.*
> (Clap baby's hands together)
> *Turn them round and round.*
> (Roll baby's hands over each other)
> *Throw them high into the air.*
> (Hold baby's hands up over his head)
> *Give a great big hug.*
> (Hold baby's arms around your neck)

Teach the song to other family members so that they can perform it with the baby. You might also sing and make up simple motions for other tunes you know. ✺

10. LEG AND FOOT MASSAGE

Age Range
9-12 months

Materials
• Baby lotion (optional)

Your baby may appreciate a breather from her busy day to relax and have her legs and feet massaged. Since a massage requires your baby's legs to be free from clothing, changing time is a good time to massage them. Before or after a bath is also a good time. Baby lotion (not oil) adds a nice touch if your baby isn't allergic to it.

While your baby is lying faceup on the changing table, begin by gently stroking her legs from her ankles to her hips. Always stroke away from her feet (and from her hands if you are massaging her arms). Be firm but gentle as you stroke. Too little pressure may tickle your baby. Too much pressure may make the muscles more tense.

Next, hold one of your baby's legs by the calf and gently bounce it up and down until you feel the muscles relax. While you are still holding her leg, squeeze and stroke

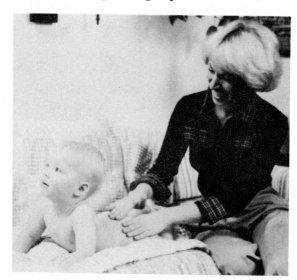

Enjoying a massage.

her thigh, knee, calf, and foot. Massage the other leg in the same way. Talk to your baby as you massage her. Tell her what you are doing and name each part of her body as you massage it: **"I'm holding your leg. Now I'm rubbing it. It feels good, doesn't it?"** Turn your baby over and massage her buttocks by moving your hands in a circular motion. Move your hands clockwise and then counterclockwise. Massage your baby's hips, thighs, knees, and calves. Gently squeeze the soles and the tops of her feet. ✖

11.   COVERING AND UNCOVERING MY EYES

Age Range
9-12 months

Materials
• None

Your active baby can make diaper-changing a bit difficult at times. It's no easy job to put diapers on a baby who insists on sitting up, turning over, and crawling over the edge of the changing table. Teach your baby the following version of peek-a-boo to amuse him while you change his diapers. In addition to having a dry bottom he will also be coordinating eye movements and hand movements, becoming a partner in play, and learning that objects continue to exist when out of sight.

Introduce the game before changing time since you need to use your hands while teaching your baby the game. Once he catches on, your hands will be free while his are kept busy. Take hold of your baby's wrists as you say, **"Let's play peek-a-boo."** Cover your baby's eyes with the palms of his hands. Wait a few seconds, then remove his hands and say, **"Peek-a-boo. I see you."** Play the game each time you

change your baby and soon he will be covering and uncovering his eyes by himself.

Your baby may "help" you peek.

To get your baby started at each changing time, you may need to cover and uncover your own eyes as an example. After showing your baby what to do, ask him to play the game: **"Cover your eyes and play peek-a-boo."** Show your baby again if necessary. He will probably enjoy seeing you cover your eyes, and he may even help you peek by tugging at your hands. ✖

12.   CHANGING-TIME RHYMES

Age Range
9-12 months

Materials
• None

Changing time can become a bore, but it doesn't have to be. When your baby is in a playful mood, take a few minutes after changing her or while dressing her to play one of the following games. There is nothing your baby will appreciate more than a few minutes of special attention from her best playmate — mom or dad.

'Round and 'Round the Garden
'Round and 'round the garden,
(Walk your fingers in a circle on baby's tummy)
Goes the Teddy Bear.
One step, two step,
(Walk your fingers toward her shoulder)
Tickle you under there.
(Tickle her under her arm)

The Lady Bug
The lady bug crawls up your arm
(Walk your fingers up baby's arm)
And sits upon your nose.
(Rest your finger on her nose)
The lady bug slides down your tummy,
(Slide your fingers down her tummy, tickling her)
And stops upon your toes.
(Wiggle her toes) 🤸

13. HANGING UP MY CLOTHES

Age Range
12-15 months

Materials
• Clothes hooks
• Laundry basket

As your baby grows older, he will want to do more and more things for himself. But where it would take you a minute to put on your baby's socks and shoes, it can take 10 to 15 if he tries to help you. Ten minutes can seem like forever when you are trying to get ready to go somewhere. But doing things for himself is an important part of his growing up. Life will be easier if you can plan a schedule that allows your baby time to do as much as he can for himself.

You can also encourage your baby to do things for himself by the way you organize his room. Place some hooks in his closet at a level that he can easily reach. When you undress him, ask him to hang up the pieces of clothing he will wear again, such as his pajamas, robe, or a pair of pants: **"You can wear these pants again tomorrow. Can you hang them on the hook?"** The first few times, you may have to walk over with him and show him how it's done. Thank him for helping: **"Good, you put the pants on the hook. Thank you for helping."** Your baby may also enjoy taking the pants off the hook the following morning when it is time to get dressed.

A lot of your baby's clothing will go straight into the laundry after one day (or less) of wear. Keep a small laundry basket on the closet floor. Ask him to put dirty clothing into the basket. Hand him one piece at a time: **"This shirt is dirty. Would you put it in the basket for me?"** Help your baby if he needs it. Then hand him another piece of clothing to put into the basket: **"Can you put your socks into the basket?"**

Let your baby hang up his towel after his bath. If you have a hook for the towel, he'll be able to hang it up easily after all his practice with clothes. You may have to lift him up to reach the hook. If you have towel racks, you'll need to show him how to hang the towel over the rack. The towel may end up in a clump sitting on top of the rack, but you can always straighten it out later if you want to. 🧍

14.　HELPING AT DRESSING TIME

Age Range
12-15 months

Materials
• None

Your baby has watched you dress her many times. Now that she's a year old she may be ready to help you — it will be the first step in learning to dress herself. At the same time she will be learning new words and coordinating the movements of her muscles.

Introduce your baby to the task of getting dressed by describing what you are doing when you dress her: **"I'm ready to put your shirt on. First, I'll put one of your arms through the sleeve. Now I'll put your other arm through the other sleeve. There, your shirt is on. Now I'm going to put on your sock, but I need your foot."** Take your baby's foot. **"Here is your foot. I'm putting your sock on your foot. Next comes your shoe. See how I slip your foot into your shoe?"** As you talk to your baby, emphasize the name of the piece of clothing you are putting on and the part of the body it goes on.

After several weeks of describing what you are doing, ask her to help you: **"I'm ready to put on your sock. Can you give me your foot?"** Take your baby's foot. **"Here is your foot."** Ask your baby to hold up her other foot so you can put the other sock on: **"Can you give me this foot** (point) **so I can put your sock on?"** If she does, let her know how clever she is: **"That's right. You gave me your foot. Good for you."** If your baby doesn't lift up her foot, lift it up for her: **"Here is your foot."**

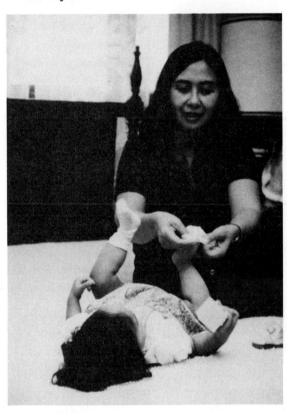

Lending a foot!

Ask your baby to give you her leg when it's time to put on pants, to give you her arm when it's time to put on a shirt, sweater, or coat, and to give you her hand when it's time to put on mittens. Before you know it, your baby will help you without your asking her to. When she does volunteer her help, always tell her how much you appreciate it. 🧍

15. DISCOVERING A FACE

Age Range
12-15 months

Materials
• None

By now your baby has probably poked at your eyes, pulled your nose, tugged on your ears, and put his fingers in your mouth many times. It's his way of learning how each part of your face feels and works. You can help your baby learn more about the face by telling him the name of each feature. Since he gazes into your face each time you diaper him, take advantage of the opportunity and teach him the names of the parts of your face.

Take your baby's hands and ask, **"Can you touch my nose?"** Touch your nose with his hands. **"That's my nose. You're touching my nose."** Make the game more entertaining by making funny faces. You can wiggle your nose or pretend to sneeze. Next, gently place your baby's hands on your eyes: **"These are my eyes."** Repeat the word *eyes* several times as your baby touches them. Talk softly and move his hands gently as he touches your eyes. When your baby touches your mouth, nibble on his fingers or kiss his hands: **"That's my mouth. You are touching my mouth. Mmm, your fingers taste good."**

Each time your baby pokes, pulls, or tugs at your face, tell him what he is poking at or pulling on. Over time he will begin to connect each facial feature with its name. You'll know that he understands when one day you ask him, "Where's my nose?" and he points to your nose without any help from you. For some ideas on how to teach your baby to point to other parts of his body, see Activity 17 of *Bathtime Business*. ✽

16. UNDERSTANDING SIMPLE OPPOSITES

Age Range
15-18 months

Materials
• Items of clothing

Up, down, on, and *off:* in order to learn these words, your baby will need to hear them and be shown what they mean many times. As you begin to stress these words in your usual conversations with your baby, you may be surprised at how many opportunities you have to use them each day.

A good time to stress the words *up* and *down* is when you are dressing your baby. When putting a shirt on over her head, ask her to raise her arm *up* so you can put it through the sleeve. Once her arm is in, ask her to put her arm *down*. Repeat when putting her other arm through the sleeve. Ask your baby to sit *down* so you can put on her socks and shoes and to stand *up* when you put on her pants. When putting on her pants, ask her to raise her leg *up* so you can put it through the pant leg. When this is accomplished, ask her to put her leg *down*. Tell your baby that you need to put her *down* so you can change her diapers.

Taking *off* a coat — with some help.

Once the job is done, describe what you are doing when you pick her *up:* **"Now you have on dry diapers. I am going to pick you up. Up, up, up you go!"**

Changing time is only one of many opportunities you'll have to stress the words *up* and *down.* Use these words whenever you pick your baby up or put her down. When you want to show her something, point and ask her to look up or to look down. Eventually she will learn the meaning of the words and understand that *up* is the opposite of *down.* She may also begin to repeat the words *up* and *down* after you. Be sure to encourage her when she does: **"Do you want to get down? Can you say 'down'? That's right, 'down.'"**

Once your baby understands *up* and *down,* you can stress the words *on* and *off* when you dress her. If she helps dress and undress herself, stress the words *on* and *off* as she takes clothing off and puts it on: **"Take your shoes *off,* (baby's name). Now take *off* your socks."** Another time: **"It's time to go outside. Put your hat on."** Once your baby understands the words *on* and *off* as they are used to describe dressing and undressing, you can stress the words in other situations. You can ask your baby to put something on the table or show her how to turn a flashlight off. ✘

17.   BRUSHING HAIR

Age Range
15-18 months

Materials
• Baby hair brush
• Unbreakable hand mirror
• Doll (optional)

There's a good chance your baby is fascinated with hair. Especially if your hair is long, little fingers can become painfully

tangled in it. Now is a good time for your baby to put his interest to constructive use by learning to brush his hair. All you need is a brush for him and a hand mirror. Keep them in the area in which you change and dress your baby.

When you have finished changing your baby, let him practice brushing his hair. Hand him the brush: **"Today you can brush your own hair."** Help him put his hand to his head and stroke his hair with the brush. Hold the mirror so he can see what he is doing. Don't forget to praise his efforts: **"Your hair looks very nice. You're doing a good job of brushing it."** In fact, your baby may be tangling his hair more than brushing it, but he *thinks* he's brushing, so he deserves your encouraging words.

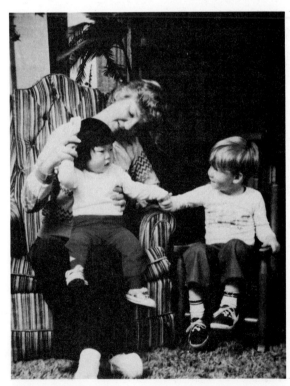

Learning to brush hair.

If you want to prevent tangles, let your baby practice on a doll. As he practices, you can give him less and less help. Soon he'll be brushing his hair by himself. Don't be surprised if your baby takes an interest in brushing the hair on any available head — especially yours! ✱

Growing with the Grass

1. Looking Around Outdoors
2. Playing with Foil
3. Studying Nature
4. Listening to a Wind Chime
5. Outdoor Sounds
6. Meeting New People
7. Looking at Bugs
8. Exploring the Outdoors
9. Handing Objects Back and Forth
10. Having a Picnic
11. Getting Acquainted with Another Baby
12. Running Errands
13. Riding on a Scooter
14. Matching Objects and Pictures
15. Swimming Pool Fun
16. Making a Nature Collage

1. LOOKING AROUND OUTDOORS

Age Range
Birth-3 months

Materials
• None

Although your baby is very young, he* will enjoy looking at objects outside. If the weather is severely cold, wait until the second month to take him out. But even in winter weather, both you and your little one can bundle up and explore the outdoors.

Hold the baby in your arms in an upright position so that he can look around as you walk. Show him brightly colored flowers, rustling leaves on the trees, his brother's or sister's outdoor toys, and anything else that he notices. In wintertime look at icicles on the bushes and buildings, sparkling snow, or reflected light on ice patches or puddles. *Talk about* things that you look at: **"You're watching the cars zooming past us. Aren't they pretty colors? There are people riding in those cars."** Stroke the baby's hand gently across some of the things he sees so that he can feel them and begin to discover textures. Don't stay out too long. When your baby begins to fuss and seems tired, end your walking and talking session until another day. ✲

---

*In odd-numbered activities, the baby is referred to as a boy. In even-numbered activities, the baby is referred to as a girl.

2. PLAYING WITH FOIL

Age Range
3-6 months

Materials
• Piece of aluminum foil

Just like everything else in her* world, the wind is something your baby must learn about. Many young babies are confused about how to breathe when they are in a heavy breeze — they gasp or suck in air very quickly. Only experience will teach your infant how to relax and breathe naturally on a windy day. You can help her relax and enjoy a breezy day outdoors by playing with a piece of aluminum foil.

Take a piece of foil outdoors with you. Even on a cold day you can bundle up and enjoy a few minutes outside. Stand in a shady area so that the foil doesn't reflect a harsh glare from the sun. You can either hold your baby while you play or put her in a playpen or stroller.

Hold the sheet of foil in front of your baby so that it rattles in the breeze. The foil will reflect different colors and make an intriguing sound as the wind shakes it. Talk to her and admire the foil: **"This foil is shiny. See all the colors on it?"** If your baby reaches for the foil, put it in her hand and let her shake it and examine it. If she brings it to her mouth, watch carefully so that she doesn't tear off small pieces and choke. NEVER LEAVE YOUR BABY ALONE WITH THE FOIL.

After she has investigated the sheet, crumple the foil into a ball (larger than 1" diameter). Toss it up and down in your hand. Let the baby hold the ball and look it over. She will want to explore its texture, taste, reflections, and sounds. ✲

---

*In even-numbered activities, the baby is referred to as a girl. In odd-numbered activities, the baby is referred to as a boy.

3. STUDYING NATURE

Age Range
3-6 months

Materials
• None

Although your baby is still very little, he is not too young to be a nature lover. Plan a scenic walk with him to a wooded park or a forest area near your home. He will be fascinated by the sights and sounds and smells around him.

Although spring and fall offer the best conditions for pleasant walking, a short winter stroll can be an enjoyable escape from the stuffy indoors. As you go along, watch your baby's face. He will probably notice trees with their rustling leaves, birds flying overhead, and squirrels racing around.

Hold him close to flowers and bushes so that he can take a look. Tickle his nose with a twig. Hold his hand on leaves, rocks, tree bark, and other textured things. Stand still and listen to birds chirping, frogs croaking, the wind whistling, and water rushing in a nearby stream. Your baby may watch everything intently or he may find the walk so relaxing that he dozes off.

4. LISTENING TO A WIND CHIME

Age Range
3-6 months

Materials
• Homemade wind chime (see below)

When you take your baby outdoors, she studies all the sounds around her. Besides the ordinary outdoor noises, you can fascinate your baby with some music from a homemade wind chime.

To make a simple wind chime you will need a clothes hanger, a yard of heavy string, and several seashells, old teaspoons, jingle bells, old keys, large common nails, or heavy nuts and bolts. To assemble the chime, cut the string into short pieces of about 5". Attach one end of each string to a shell or other object. You might tie, glue, or tape the string to the object. Then tie the other end of the string to the horizontal bar on the hanger. Hang all of the objects from the hanger in this way. They should be close to each other so that they touch and make clinking noises when you hold up the hanger. Hang your wind chime from a low branch of a tree, or a nail or hook on a porch.

Taking a breather.

Hold your baby near the wind chime so that she can see it move while she listens to the clinking sounds. Put her hand on the swaying chimes and talk to her: **"Feel the pretty shells. They're making music for you."** ✗

5. OUTDOOR SOUNDS

Age Range
6-9 months

Materials
• None

Outdoor time is learning time for your baby. When you take him for a walk in a stroller, he learns a great deal about the sights, sounds, and smells of your neighborhood. Whether you live in a rural area, a suburb, or a city, you can draw your baby's attention to many fascinating outdoor sounds.

Try taking familiar noisemakers with you when you go outdoors.

While you push your baby in a stroller or carriage, listen for sounds around you. There are many noises that you ordinarily don't notice because they are so familiar to you. These might include traffic sounds, animal sounds, sounds from machinery, or sounds created by the wind. To draw your baby's attention to a particular sound, stop walking and turn him toward the source of the sound. Then imitate the sound and name it for him: *"Rrrrr.* **That's a truck, (baby's name).** *Rrrr.* **Truck."** Give your baby plenty of time to focus on the sound.

Of course, if there are many distractions your baby may not notice the sound at all. If possible, move closer to it and turn his head directly toward it. He may notice other sounds on his own. If he turns toward a noise, imitate it for him and name it. Then let him listen. ✷

6. MEETING NEW PEOPLE

Age Range
6-9 months

Materials
• None

By this time your baby may begin to fear strangers or even a friendly relative that she sees only occasionally. Try not to lose patience with your baby if she seems to be afraid of everyone. If you put her in pleasant situations where she sees new people, she will eventually overcome her fear. To help her, plan a trip to a nearby park with someone your baby doesn't know well. By spending friendly time with this person, she will gradually relax and enjoy being with the new person.

Take several trips to the park alone with your baby before you invite someone else to come along. In that way, she will get to know the park and feel comfortable there. Before your guest arrives, tell your baby the person's name and explain several times that he or she will be visiting. Then your baby will be familiar with the sound of that person's name. **"We're having a visitor. (Sandy) is coming over. Sandy wants to play with you at the park. Sandy is very nice."**

When the visitor arrives, act very friendly to relieve any anxiety your baby might feel about this person. Then have your guest say hello to your baby while you hold her. Hold you baby's hand toward your guest and let them shake hands. If your baby seems relaxed, see if she will let this new person hold her. But don't force the issue, especially if she seems frightened.

Walk to the park together and carry on a lively conversation with your friend. Address your baby once in a while so that she feels included. At the park ask your friend to push your baby in a baby swing. If your baby is willing, she and your friend might go down the slide or ride on the see-saw. With lots of gentle persuasion your baby might even like this new person by the time the visit is over. ✷

7. LOOKING AT BUGS

Age Range
6-9 months

Materials
• Bugs

When you are outdoors, your baby probably notices the neighborhood pets and wild animals. But don't forget the bugs! Bugs will also fascinate your baby. If the weather is warm, you can easily find some crawly creatures for him to examine.

Your baby will have no fear of the bugs he encounters. If you are squeamish about bugs yourself, choose "nice" insects to show your baby, such as ladybugs, fireflies, or ants. When you find a bug, hold it in your hand for your baby to see. Talk about the bug and admire it: **"Look at this tiny ladybug. She's crawling on my finger."**

Put the bug on your baby's arm or the back of his hand. Be careful that he doesn't pop the unfortunate bug into his mouth! Watch the bug with your baby and talk about what the bug is doing: **"It's trying to crawl off your arm. Maybe she'll jump onto the grass. There she goes!"** ✷

8. EXPLORING THE OUTDOORS

Age Range
9-12 months

Materials
- Stroller
- Items found outdoors

The outdoors offers a fascinating world of things to see, hear, smell, and feel. Now that your baby is older, she can begin to participate actively in outdoor explorations. All you need is a well-rested baby, a stroller, and a sunny day.

Exploring leaves on an autumn day.

Point out trees, flowers, and other plant life as you walk along. Pick leaves off different types of trees. Give them to your baby to hold and examine. (Watch to make sure she doesn't put them in her mouth.) Pick a flower or two for your baby to look at. Sniff the flower and hold it under her nose so she can smell it, too. Pick a dandelion that has turned from flower to fluff and blow it into the air. Let your baby try to blow one. Name the colors of some of the plants you see. If you find a nut under a tree, shake it to see if it rattles. Then hand it to your baby (but keep it away from her mouth, especially if it is small).

Take your baby out of her stroller and let her feel the roughness of pavement and of tree bark. Tickle her with a blade of grass.

If there is a breeze, talk about how the wind feels and how it is blowing your hair or the leaves on the trees. Find a smooth stone for your baby to feel.

Your baby will not understand many of the things you talk about. But showing her the things around her during a walk will help her to learn the names of things and to distinguish colors and textures. ✱

9. HANDING OBJECTS BACK AND FORTH

Age Range
9-12 months

Materials
- Items found outdoors

Teaching your baby the meaning of the phrase "Give it to (Mommy)" can pay off at times. It may come in handy when he has picked up something dirty or small enough to swallow, or when he has picked up the vase Aunt Diane gave you which is not only breakable but half his size. A simple and delightful game can help your baby learn the meaning of the phrase.

When sitting outside with your baby, find an object that he is familiar with. If you use something new to your baby, he may find it so intriguing that he won't be willing to give it up. Look for a flower, a leaf, or a colorful stone. Or use keys if you happen to have them with you.

Hand the object to your baby and say, **"Here is a flower, (baby's name). Take the flower."** Your baby will probably be most cooperative. If necessary, put the flower into his hand. Pause a few moments and then ask for the flower back: **"Can I have the flower? Give me the flower."** Reach for the flower and "encourage" your baby to hand it to you. Once the flower is back in your hand you can smell it, talk about how pretty it is, or comment on its color. Then give the object back to your baby and say, **"Take the flower, (baby's name)."** You can add a lesson in courtesy to this game by saying please and thank you.

After several rounds of this game you may feel it is a bit monotonous. But keep it up as long as your baby is interested. He'll let you know when he has had enough. ✦

Helping out in the garden.

10. HAVING A PICNIC

  Age Range
  9-12 months

  Materials
  • Baby cup and spoon
  • Food and drink

Occasionally add a special touch to your noon meal by eating outside under a tree or on your front step. It will be a nice change of pace for both you and your baby. Fresh air and sunshine can perk you up in the middle of the day. A bonus to eating outside is the easy cleanup afterward.

Since you don't have to worry about spilling when eating outside, a "picnic" is a good opportunity for your baby to practice drinking from a cup. There are several kinds of cups to choose from. Some have handles and some don't. Some cups have lids that limit the flow of liquid. See-through cups help you to tell if your baby is tipping the cup back far enough to get the liquid to her mouth. You can also tell when the liquid is gone.

Fill the cup about half full of water, juice, or milk. Your baby might not drink all the liquid, but this way she won't have to tip the cup very far back to get the liquid to her mouth. If she needs help, guide her hands as she lifts the cup to her mouth. If the cup doesn't have a lid on it, expect some spills. Your baby may choke occasionally as she gets used to the cup. If she chokes often, she probably isn't quite ready to drink from a cup that doesn't have a lid. As with everything else, the more your baby practices drinking from a cup, the less you will have to help her. She will also choke and spill less.

You can also give your baby practice eating from a spoon if you include cottage cheese or macaroni and cheese in her lunch. Or have a special snack outside, such as ice cream or yogurt. Help your baby wrap her fingers around the spoon. Guide her hand as she picks up some of the food and then guide her hand to her mouth. Give your baby less and less help until she is able to put the spoon in her mouth by herself. It will probably take her longer to learn how to scoop the food than how to put the spoon in her mouth. Give your baby lots of encouragement as she is learning to feed herself. ✦

11. GETTING ACQUAINTED WITH ANOTHER BABY

Age Range
9-12 months

Materials
- Toys: 2 balls, 2 trucks, 2 dolls

Getting out with your baby can be good for both of you. The outing can be turned into a social event by arranging to meet another parent and baby. The babies will benefit from the opportunity to play with each other. You will also benefit from being able to visit with another parent. Of course, playing together at this age may consist of staring at each other, poking at each other's face, or sitting side by side, each with his own toy. But even these early meetings are important because they help your baby get to know other people. As he gets older, he will begin to learn some of the rules necessary for getting along with others.

A playground is a good place to take the babies to play side by side. Take some toys along, making sure you have two of each toy. At the playground you can push the babies in the swings, or seat them next to each other. Be sure to hold on to your baby as you push him around. The babies may also enjoy the teeter-totter. Hold on to them as you gently push them up and down. Seat the babies next to each other in the grass. Give them each a similar toy to play with. It will be interesting to watch how they play together. Each may just play on his own. Or they may play together or imitate each other. Don't be surprised if there is a squabble over the toys. You can help to resolve it by making sure each baby has a similar toy: **"This is your truck, (Kevin). And this truck is (Eric's)."** If possible, plan regular get-togethers with your baby and another baby, either indoors or out. ✶

12. RUNNING ERRANDS

Age Range
12-15 months

Materials
- Household or outdoor items: hotpad, flower, leaf, or unbreakable dish

This activity will keep your baby busy when you are outside with your family working in the yard, having a barbecue, or just enjoying the sunshine. It will give your baby practice if she is beginning to walk. It also teaches her to follow directions. Although it is very simple, your baby may find it quite enjoyable.

The activity encourages your baby to walk from you to another family member — what could be simpler? To give a little more meaning to your baby's journey, ask her to carry something and deliver it to the other person. Be sure the object is completely safe, in case she falls with it. For example, if you are barbecuing, you might ask your baby to deliver a hotpad. If you are working in the yard, ask her to carry a flower or leaf.

Give the object to your baby and ask her to take it to someone nearby. If she has to walk too far to deliver the object, she may lose interest along the way. Point to the person and say, **"Take the flower to (Daddy). Can you give the flower to Daddy?"** Dad can help make the activity a success by standing with outstretched arms and calling to the baby, **"Come to me, (baby's name). Bring the flower to Daddy."** Of course, when your baby does deliver the object, Dad should make a big fuss over it: **"What a beautiful flower. It smells very nice. Thank you. Now take the flower back to (Mommy)."** Don't be surprised if you find your baby carrying the object back and forth between you several times. After all the warm praise you gave your child, you can't blame her! ✶

13. RIDING ON A SCOOTER

Age Range
12-15 months

Materials
• Scooter

Your baby may welcome a change from being pushed in his stroller. You can give him this change by letting him ride on a scooter. Your baby is ready for a scooter once he begins to walk. If he begins walking in the dead of winter, he can learn to ride the scooter indoors. By the time the weather is nice and you turn him loose outside, he'll probably be riding like a pro. There are a variety of riding toys available that are made to look like trucks, horses, or cars. Keep in mind that it is harder to control the toys that have a steering wheel.

When you first give your baby the scooter, let him have lots of time to explore it. If it is a car with a horn, show him how to beep it. If it's shaped like a horse, show him how to make it whinny. At first your baby may prefer to walk while holding on to the toy. If so, he may enjoy giving his favorite doll or teddy bear a ride. When he is ready to sit in the driver's seat, encourage him to push off with his feet. He is as likely to go backward as forward, so always be nearby just in case he loses his balance.

To help your baby get going on his own, lift both of his feet slightly, put them down, and push against the floor. Then lift them up again. Some babies prefer to "walk" the toy forward by pushing off with each foot alternately. Encourage your baby whichever way he uses. ✖

14. MATCHING OBJECTS AND PICTURES

Age Range
15-18 months

Materials
• Pictures or photographs of outdoor items
• Construction paper or poster board (optional)

As you and your baby spend time together outside, she will become familiar with the names of many of the things she sees. When you look at picture books together she sees some of the same things — trees, rocks, flowers, grass, houses, leaves, and cars. This activity helps your baby associate outdoor objects with pictures of those objects. You can also include pictures of toys she uses outside, such as a bucket and shovel, a wagon, and a ball. If you like, paste each picture onto a piece of construction paper or poster board.

Take three of the pictures along when you go outside with your baby. Walk around the yard and find the things in the pictures. Show your baby the picture of the object: **"Look, (baby's name). This is a flower."** Then point to the real flower: **"This is a flower, too."** Point again to the picture and then to the flower, naming it each time. If the object is small enough, let your baby hold it. Then hold the picture next to the object and ask her, **"Where is the flower?"** Praise her if she points to either the picture or the flower. **"That's right. That's a flower. This is a flower also."** Show your baby the two other pictures using the procedure described above.

After several weeks of showing your baby objects and pictures of objects, she may be ready to play a matching game. Find an object she is familiar with. If possible, let her hold it. Then show your baby two pictures; one of the pictures should be a picture of the object you have given her. Say to her, **"Point to the rock. Where is the rock?"** Give her time to point to the right picture. If she isn't sure what to do, point to the rock and say, **"Rock."** Take your baby's finger and help her point to the picture of the rock. Say "Rock" again. Let your baby play with the rock and the picture. Repeat the game using other pictures and matching objects.

This game can be played indoors as well as outdoors. Use objects you have inside that your baby is familiar with — for example, a spoon, cup, brush, chair, or doll. ✦

15. SWIMMING POOL FUN

Age Range
15-18 months

Materials
- 2 plastic boats
- Plastic stacking rings
- 8-10 floatable objects
- Plastic bowl
- Inflatable pool (optional)

There are few things your baby would appreciate more on a hot summer day than a cool dip in a swimming pool. If you invite another baby (and parent) and select the right toys, fun in the pool can also be a lesson in sharing. A small, inflatable plastic pool can provide hours of fun during the summer, so you may want to consider purchasing one. But the activity can be done just as successfully in the baby area at the public pool.

Seat the babies in the pool, facing each other. Put some of the toys between them and let them play in their own way for a while. Then try one or several of the following ideas to encourage the babies to play together. Give one of the babies a

plastic boat. Show him how to push the boat through the water to the other baby. Then show that baby how to push the boat back. Encourage them to push the boat back and forth several times: **"(Melissa), can you push the boat to (Johnny)? That's the way. Now Johnny has it. Johnny, you push the boat to Melissa. Nice job!"** If one of the babies doesn't want to give up the boat, don't force him. Give the spare boat to the other baby to play with.

Put the plastic stacking rings in front of the babies. Hold the largest one in between them. Show them how to put a ring on top of the one you are holding. Encourage them to build a tower by taking turns. They may get only one ring on before it topples or is knocked over, but that's part of the fun.

Place the plastic bowl between the babies. Dump the floating objects into the pool. Ask the babies to pick up the objects and put them into the bowl. You can add some fun to the game by encouraging them to put the objects into the bowl quickly: **"Let's see how fast you can put all these Ping-Pong balls into the bowl. Pick that one up. Hurry. There's another one. Get that one. You're doing it so quickly. Good for you."** If the babies enjoy the game, dump the objects into the water and play it again. ✦

Note: Because drowning is the second leading cause of accidental death among children aged 1-5, *never* leave a baby more than an arm's length from a watchful adult. This rule holds no matter how little water there is in the pool.

16. MAKING A NATURE COLLAGE

Age Range
15-18 months

Materials
- Nontoxic paste
- Plain paper or cardboard
- Items for collage (see below)

Your baby may be ready to enjoy pasting items onto paper. She can do everything with paste that she would like to do with her mashed potatoes. But unlike mashed potatoes, paste makes things stick together. So your baby will not only be learning about paste but may also end up with a lovely collage. The collage may have only one or two items on it. But her biggest fan — you — will naturally think it's a masterpiece.

Collages can be made with scraps of wrapping paper and fabric, pieces of ribbon and yarn, empty spools of thread, cotton balls, and pictures cut from catalogs. Items you find outdoors make a very special collage. To make a nature collage you will also need a sheet of plain paper or cardboard and some nontoxic paste. Since you or your baby won't always be able to control where the paste will land, you may also want to dress her in old clothes.

Take your baby on a short walk to gather things for the collage. Leaves, flowers, sticks, stones, nutshells, feathers, and small pine cones (all larger than 1" diameter) can all be used in a collage. Since this is your baby's first experience with paste, she may be more interested in getting acquainted with the paste than in making a collage. So you don't need to collect many items.

If the weather is nice, make the collage outside on a patio, the sidewalk, or a driveway. Being outdoors makes an appropriate backdrop for the activity. You will also be more relaxed if you don't have to worry about spills. If you are working inside, set up the activity in an area that can easily be cleaned. Introduce the activity to your baby by reminding her of the walk you took earlier: **"Remember when we walked around the yard and found these pretty things?"** Pick up and name some of the items you found: **"We found a flower, a stick, and a rock. You're going to make a pretty picture with these things."** Show your baby the paste: **"This is paste. Watch me."** Put some paste on your finger and then spread the paste on an object. Paste the object to the paper. **"I put paste on the flower so the flower will stick to the paper. You put paste on something."** Your baby will probably need lots of help. She may be more interested in feeling (and tasting) the paste than in making a collage. If she manages to get one or two things pasted onto the paper, she is off to a good start. Give her lots of encouragement. ✶

A Classroom in the Kitchen

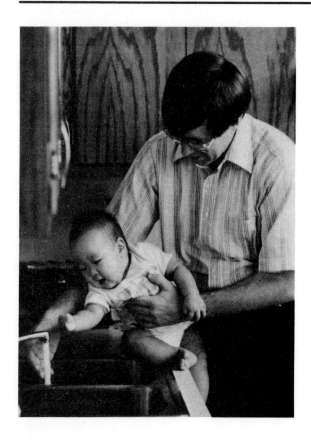

1. Listening to a Song
2. Listening to Kitchen Sounds
3. Listening and Looking in the Kitchen
4. Pulling
5. Feeling Textures
6. Moving Around
7. Exploring Objects
8. Making Sounds
9. Hitting Pots and Pans
10. Magnets
11. Removing Objects from a Container
12. Fun in the Kitchen Cabinet
13. Learning New Words
14. Dropping Objects into a Bottle
15. Sniffing in the Kitchen
16. Nesting Bowls
17. Fixing Dinner
18. Setting the Table

1. LISTENING TO A SONG

Age Range
Birth-3 months

Materials
• None

Singing is a pleasant way to communicate love and closeness to your baby. Infants enjoy listening to songs as much as everyone else. A soft, slow song can soothe an upset baby; a snappy, happy tune can bring a delightful first smile to his* face. When you sing to your young baby, he will appreciate your songs no matter what kind of voice you have.

Take time-out to have a chat.

Clean-up time in the kitchen is a good opportunity for a concert. Seat the baby in an infant seat and either strap the seat into a high chair or place it next to you on the floor.

As you wash dishes or prepare them for the dishwasher, sing simple tunes that you remember from your own childhood. These might include "Twinkle, Twinkle, Little Star," "The Farmer in the Dell," or "Mary Had a Little Lamb." You might also sing popular songs, or religious songs, opera, or your favorite folk tunes. Look at your infant as often as you can while you sing to let him sense that you're singing for him. Enjoy your baby's response. He might smile, wiggle, coo, or simply stare in wonder as you sing your songs. ✘

2. LISTENING TO KITCHEN SOUNDS

Age Range
Birth-3 months

Materials
• Kitchen utensils and appliances

From the first days of life, your baby is sensitive to sound. Noises will fascinate her* and hold her attention easily. While you are putting away dishes after a meal, you can introduce your little one to a variety of sounds.

Place the baby near you in an infant seat, cradle, or playpen. Before you put away dishes, pots and pans, eating utensils and glasses, hold them near the baby and make noises with them. For example, you might hit the side of a glass with a spoon, quietly clap two pan lids together, run a spatula along the ridges of a grater, or click a pair of tongs open and shut. As long as your

*In odd-numbered activities, the baby is referred to as a boy. In even-numbered activities, the baby is referred to as a girl.

*In even-numbered activities, the baby is referred to as a girl. In odd-numbered activities, the baby is referred to as a boy.

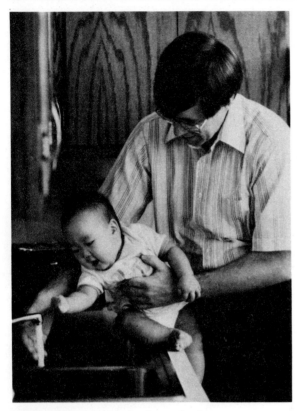

Listening to (and touching) a stream of water..

baby is not overwhelmed, she will enjoy listening to the sounds and watching the objects that produce them.

After the dishes are put away, hold your infant and introduce her to other kitchen sounds. You might turn on a can opener or a blender, ring a timer, run water in the sink, or turn on a vent fan or garbage disposal. Some of the sounds may scare her. If so, comfort her and then introduce softer noises. As you explore the kitchen with your baby, you will probably hear sounds that even you don't notice every day. ✳

3. LISTENING AND LOOKING IN THE KITCHEN

Age Range
Birth-3 months

Materials
• Kitchen utensils
• Foods

Meal preparation can be a frantic time of day, especially if your baby wants attention while you're trying to get dinner on the table. If your baby is willing to sit in his infant seat while you work, you can share some time with him and still prepare a delicious meal.

An older baby will enjoy watching you from an exercise chair.

Put the baby near you in his infant seat (but not on a counter). While you cut vegetables, make a salad, or peel potatoes, talk to him about what you're doing: **"I'm cutting these carrots into little pieces. Then I'll cook them for our supper. See**

this piece of carrot? It's orange, and it tastes sweet." Hold up pieces of food and utensils for the baby to see. He will enjoy the various colors and shapes as well as the reflected light from metal and glassware.

4. PULLING

Age Range
3-6 months

Materials
- Piece of elastic, tape, small object (see below)

As your baby reaches out to touch the things around her, she will discover that she can cause changes in her world. She can make things move and produce sounds, and she can even change their shape. Using a piece of elastic, some tape, and an attractive object, you can make a simple plaything for your baby to pull on and manipulate while you are busy in the kitchen.

Cut a strip of elastic about 6" long. Tape one end of the elastic securely to the object. It might be a small ball, a colorful key holder, a large jingle bell (larger than 1" diameter), a teething ring, or a plastic medicine bottle filled with rice and tightly capped. If possible, use an object that makes noise. Tape the other end of the elastic to your kitchen table so that the object hangs about 12" above the floor.

Place the baby in her infant seat and put the seat under the hanging object. If she doesn't reach for the object and grab it, put it into her hand. Hold her hand while she grasps the object, and pull down until you feel tension on the elastic. Then let go of your baby's hand. If she lets go of the object, she can watch it "dance" around. If she pulls on it, she will enjoy feeling the tension of the elastic. As she plays with the hanging toy, your baby will discover that she is the one who is causing it to move. She might bat it, grab it, pull it toward her mouth, or shake it vigorously. After a while, attach a different object to the piece of elastic.

5. FEELING TEXTURES

Age Range
3-6 months

Materials
- Container
- Assorted objects with different textures: measuring spoons, washcloth, greeting card, ball of tape (all larger than 1" diameter)

Once your baby is able to hold objects in his hands, he will also begin to put everything into his mouth. As long as the objects are safe and reasonably clean, there is no need to worry. This is one way for the baby to explore objects — how they feel and taste, and what kind of shape they have. While you are working in the kitchen, your baby can explore a variety of objects with his hands and mouth. On your kitchen counter keep a container filled with interesting objects. Try to include things with different textures — rough, smooth, bumpy, spongy, soft, and hard.

Before you prepare a meal, set the table, clear the dishes, sweep the floor, or do

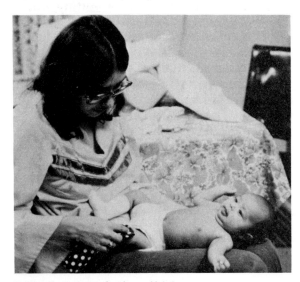

Feeling the texture of a piece of fabric.

some other kitchen job, place your baby near you in an infant seat. Then hand him one object from the container of things. Let him explore the object by holding it, tasting it, shaking it, and looking at it. Talk to him about it: **"I bet that washcloth tastes good. Do you feel the little bumps in the terrycloth?"** After a short while, put the first object back into the container and give your baby another item to examine. If you change the objects frequently, your baby may stay happily busy while you do your kitchen work.

6. MOVING AROUND

Age Range
3-6 months

Materials
- Colorful object: unbreakable bowl or cup, empty cracker box, or dish towel

Crawling is a skill that your baby will learn on her own, but you can help her get ready for the big event with a challenging floor activity. Your baby can do this exercise on her own while you are busy in the kitchen.

Place your baby on her tummy on the kitchen floor. Then find an attractive object that is safe for her to handle. Put it on the floor in front of her and a little to one side. Stoop down next to the object and try to spark her interest in it: **"Look at this pretty striped towel. See if you can get it."** If your baby attempts to reach for the object in any way (by waving her arms wildly or rocking her body with excitement), hand it to her with lots of praise: **"That's the way! You almost got it yourself."**

After your baby explores the object for a while, take it away and place something else near her. This time leave your baby alone while you work nearby. As she turns and reaches toward the object, she'll be exercising the arm and leg muscles that she will soon use to creep and then crawl.

Once your baby can reach for and retrieve something that is slightly to one side, make the activity more challenging. Place an object farther down along her side. Make sure that she sees it, and then leave her alone to pivot her body around and grab the object. ✶

Reaching for a fabric block.

7. EXPLORING OBJECTS

Age Range
6-9 months

Materials
• Homemade shakers (see below)

By now your baby spends every waking moment actively exploring his world. As he studies what he sees, he learns about size, shape, and color. By handling things, he learns about dimension and weight. He sorts out different sounds that he hears, and of course he gives everything the taste test. While you are busy working in your kitchen, offer your baby a variety of homemade shakers to examine and enjoy.

To make each shaker, fill an empty container with rice, dried beans, sand, buttons, gravel, water, or anything else. Use unbreakable containers with lids that you can seal securely. You might use plastic margarine tubs, plastic beverage bottles, medicine bottles, coffee cans with tightly fitting plastic lids, or plastic baby bottles. Fill some of the containers only slightly and others to varying degrees. Make sure the lids are tightly taped or glued to prevent the baby from getting into the small, potentially dangerous things inside.

Seat your baby in his high chair and place the shakers on the tray so that he can explore them freely. The various shakers will have different shapes for him to examine. Some will be lightweight and others will feel heavy. They will make different sounds when he shakes them. They will have different patterns and colors for him to study. And they will all make a delightful *bang* when he drops them on the floor. ✶

8. MAKING SOUNDS

Age Range
6-9 months

Materials
• None

Your baby may be saying certain sounds over and over — sounds like *ma, da,* or *ba.* Or there may be certain babbles or gurgles that she enjoys making. While you are busy in the kitchen you can listen to your baby and respond to these beginning speech sounds.

Put your baby in her high chair close to where you are working. Give her plenty of toys so that she'll play while you work. As you work, listen carefully to the sounds she makes. Then look at her and imitate one or two of her favorites. From time to time, make one of these sounds and see if she will repeat it. After your baby says the sound several times, say a different sound. See if she'll repeat that one. This may spark a lively exchange between the two of you. It may also inspire your baby to make up a new sound or two.

Reward your baby for saying sounds that resemble words. For example, whenever your baby says "ma," you might reply, **"I'm over here. I'm ma-ma."** Or if your baby says "ka-ka," you might hand her a cup and say, **"Here's a cup. Cup."** Although at first your baby will not associate the sounds she makes with words that have meaning, eventually she will begin to connect certain sounds with persons ("da-da"), things ("ba-ba" for a toy bear), or events ("na-na" for "good night"). ✶

9. HITTING POTS AND PANS

Age Range
6-9 months

Materials
• Plastic spatula or wooden stirring spoons
• Pot or pan

Kitchen utensils will make excellent playthings for your child well into his toddler years. While you are busy cooking or cleaning up, let him drum on pots and pans to create a kitchen concert for you.

Pots and pans sound fine in the living room, too.

Seat your baby in his high chair and hand him a plastic spatula or a large wooden spoon. Let him play with the utensil for a while, but keep an eye on him so that he doesn't hurt himself. Then place a pot or pan in front of him and help him hit it with the utensil: **"Listen. You can make a noise on this pot.** *Bang!* **What a great sound."**

Give your baby a chance to hit the pot by himself. If he doesn't hit the pot with the spatula or spoon, help him do it several times. Then go about your kitchen work and let your baby hit the pot or play with it in any other way that he likes. If he does hit the pot, compliment him on his music: **"That sounds terrific. Can I hear more?"**

If you have other children, hand each of them a pot or pan and a spoon. Ask them to join the baby's concert. ✡

10. MAGNETS

Age Range
9-12 months

Materials
• Magnets (larger than 1" diameter)

Your baby may keep quite busy with this simple activity. It is a good way to give her some practice coordinating eye and hand movements. All you need is a refrigerator door and several magnets. Keep in mind that some decorative magnets are not safe to use because they have small items glued onto them that your baby could break off and swallow.

When you're together in the kitchen, seat your baby in front of the refrigerator. Remove one of the magnets from the refrigerator door, hold it for a second, and then place it back on the door. Talk to your child as you handle the magnet: **"This is a magnet. I am going to take it off the refrigerator. Look. I can put it back on the door and it will stay there."** Let your baby experiment with the magnets as you get on with your work in the kitchen. She may find that putting the magnets on the refrigerator is a bit more difficult than taking them off. But the problem is easily solved if you are occasionally willing to put them back for her. ✡

11. REMOVING OBJECTS FROM A CONTAINER

Age Range
9-12 months

Materials
• Apron with pocket
• Measuring spoon, napkin ring, cracker, small box, or other small item

Your baby may be underfoot at times when you are working in the kitchen. Rather than shooing him away, try this activity. It allows him to be with you, but not in your way. He'll also be getting some practice coordinating hand and finger movements by removing objects from a container. The objects are "surprises" from your kitchen cabinets. The container is a pocket on your apron.

Seat your baby in his high chair near a counter where you are working. Put on the apron so your baby can reach into the pocket while you are standing next to him. You may have to tie the apron under your arms or around your neck rather than around your waist.

Then place an object in the apron pocket. Don't let him see the object as you place it in your pocket. If you are making some gelatin, use the empty box, or use a measuring spoon if you are baking. A cucumber slice or cracker is a special surprise if your baby is getting hungry, and dinner is going to be late. You can also keep a basket of a few small toys in your kitchen for this and other activities.

Say, **"There's a surprise for you in my pocket. Let's see what it is."** Remove the object from the pocket. **"It's a cucumber slice!"** Place the object back in your pocket while your baby is watching you. Ask him, **"Can you take the slice out of my pocket?"**

Let your baby play with the object once he has taken it from your pocket. When he's no longer interested in it, slip something else into your pocket and continue the game. 🤸

12.   FUN IN THE KITCHEN CABINET

Age Range
9-12 months

Materials
• Cabinet stocked with safe kitchen items

Your baby thinks that you are terrific, so it's no wonder she wants to be near you so much of the time. You represent love and security to her. Consider it a compliment rather than a nuisance when your baby wants to be held while you're fixing dinner or doing the dishes. It's just her way of saying, "I love you, need you, and want to be close to you." You aren't the first and won't be the last parent to fix meals one-handed.

A baby and a safe kitchen cabinet go together well!

There are going to be times, however, when it will be impossible to hold your baby while working in the kitchen. One solution is to stock a kitchen cabinet just for her pleasure. This allows you to get your work done, and it helps teach your baby how to play by herself.

Select a low cabinet and put things in it that will be safe for your baby to play with. Try pots and pans with lids, plastic containers with lids, measuring spoons and cups, a wooden spoon, and dish towels. If you don't have duplicates of these items, it may throw off the organization of your kitchen; but take heart, it's only temporary. (Perhaps this is a good time to reorganize a bit, anyway?) Move things that could be harmful to your child, such as cleaning supplies, sharp items, and glass items, to cabinets out of her reach. Select a cabinet away from the stove for your baby's use. You may want her to play only in "her" cabinet, making all others off limits. Use safety locks to make sure she won't get into the other cabinets.

When you're together in the kitchen, show your baby the cabinet you have prepared for her. Chances are, she will take it from there. Or if you like, take a few items out of the cabinet to get her started. Put a lid on one of the pots, bang the wooden spoon on one of the pans, or play a quick game of peek-a-boo with the towel. Your baby may find opening and closing the cabinet door as much fun as playing with the things inside. To keep the cabinet interesting, change some of the items in it every week or two. Don't forget to comment from time to time on what your baby is doing and to occasionally throw a smile and kiss her way. ✳

13. LEARNING NEW WORDS

Age Range
12-15 months

Materials
• Kitchen items or foods

Your baby will learn to talk by hearing other people talk. Since you and your baby are often together, it is likely he will learn many of his first words from you. Some words he will "pick up" as he listens to you talk. As he's learning, you can give him a boost by showing him the things you are talking about and by teaching him new words.

Listening to your baby is as important as talking to him. Whenever possible, look at your baby when he is "talking" and repeat some of the sounds he is making. Teach him words that contain some of the sounds he is already making. For instance, if your baby is saying "m-m-m" he might be ready to learn the word *milk*. When selecting a word to teach your baby, make sure it is easy to say and interesting or useful. For example, he may find the word *ball* interesting and the word *milk* useful. Since many of the things familiar to your baby are in the kitchen, it is a good place to teach him a few new words.

When you are together in the kitchen, decide on a word to teach your baby. If you have chosen the word *spoon*, show him a spoon. Then use the word in several simple sentences: **"This is a spoon. You eat with a spoon."** Hold the spoon near your face so your baby can see your mouth move as you say the word. Then give him the spoon and say the word again.

Try to find an opportunity to show your baby the spoon and to say the word at least twice a day. A natural time to "work on" the word *spoon* is while you are feeding your baby or doing the dishes. At some

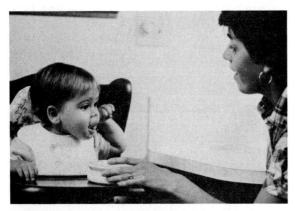
An appropriate time to teach the word *spoon.*

point your baby will make a sound after hearing you say "spoon." It may take a stretch of the imagination to say that he actually spoke the word *spoon,* but to your baby that's exactly what he did! Show your delight by saying, **"Yes! It is a spoon."** It may take a month or more before your baby says something that sounds like "spoon." Meanwhile, what is important is that you encourage him to talk and that you listen to him when he does. ✖

14. DROPPING OBJECTS INTO A BOTTLE

Age Range
12-15 months

Materials
- Plastic baby bottle
- 12 cereal bits on small plate

As your baby has grown over the past months, you've watched her develop in many ways. Around your baby's second month her small-muscle control consisted of swiping at an object or holding it for a few seconds. Now your baby can easily pick up and hold a small object between her thumb and forefinger. As your baby continues to grow, she will develop more control over her small muscles. This

activity is designed to give her practice at coordinating hand and eye movements. It has a side benefit of keeping her busy as you work in the kitchen.

Seat your baby on the floor. Place the bottle between her legs and put the plate next to the bottle. Pick up a cereal bit and drop it into the bottle as you describe to your baby what you are doing: **"I am picking up a cereal bit and dropping it into the bottle."** Pick up another cereal bit and drop it into the bottle. Ask her to try it — if she hasn't already begun to imitate you. If she seems puzzled, guide her hand to the cereal bits and hand her one. Then guide her hand over to the bottle and help her let go of the cereal. Watch to see if your baby will try the activity on her own. If not, help her one more time. As she catches on, you can leave her to the activity and go back to your work.

As a variation, ask your baby to put a cereal bit into your mouth.

For obvious reasons, you won't want to try this activity with a hungry baby. She won't understand why you would want her to put perfectly good cereal bits into a bottle when it is much more satisfying to put them into her mouth. Even if you do the activity with a baby who has just eaten, you may find fewer cereal bits at the end of the activity than you had at the beginning. ✖

15.   SNIFFING IN THE KITCHEN

Age Range
12-15 months

Materials
• Foods

Your baby is learning to identify the objects in the world around him. He will get acquainted with these things by looking at them and handling them. You may have a baby who also likes to give everything the taste test. This activity cultivates one of your baby's other senses — his sense of smell. What better place to have a lesson on sniffing than in the kitchen, where some of our favorite smells are found! You don't need any special materials for this activity — just your baby by your side as you are preparing a meal.

When you're together in the kitchen, seat your baby near you in his high chair. When handling different foods, name them for him: **"This is a lemon."** Sniff the item. **"Mmm, it smells good."** Hold the food under your baby's nose and ask him to smell it. It may take some practice before he breathes in to smell the food. Always sniff the items yourself to show him what to do.

The items your baby can sniff in the kitchen are endless. He can smell the bar of soap you use for washing your hands, or the vanilla you use when baking. Let your baby smell the bread, peanut butter, and jelly you use when making a sandwich, or the fruits you are slicing for a salad. Call your baby's attention to the smells in the air made by something baking in the oven. Sniff the air: **"Mmm, it smells good in here. I smell the apple pie baking."** 🧍

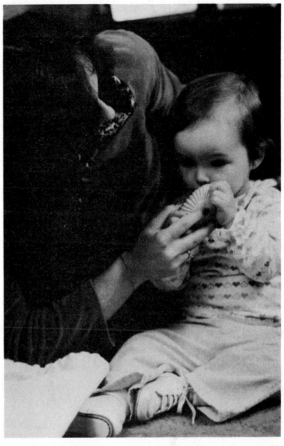

Smelling a bar of soap.

16. NESTING BOWLS

Age Range
15-18 months

Materials
- Plastic or metal mixing bowls or measuring cups

While browsing through toy stores you may have noticed "nesting" cups — cups of different sizes that fit inside one another. Making a nest of containers is a good problem-solving activity for your baby. The set of plastic or metal mixing bowls or measuring cups you use for cooking can easily become a set of nesting cups for your baby.

When you are together in the kitchen, seat your baby on the floor. Put three mixing bowls inside one another and place them in front of her. Get her attention and slowly remove the small bowl and place it on the floor. Next, remove the middle-sized bowl and place it on the floor. Pause and then place the middle-sized bowl back inside the large bowl and place the small bowl inside the middle-sized bowl.

Take the bowls apart again and ask your baby to fit them back together: **"Now you put the bowls together."** If she hesitates, take her hand and guide her through the steps of putting the bowls together. Take the bowls apart one more time and let your baby experiment with them on her own. Don't be discouraged if she decides to use the bowls as cymbals or as a hat rather than as nesting cups. Fitting the bowls together will take some practice. Whenever you have an opportunity, get out the bowls and demonstrate how they fit inside one another. Sooner or later your baby will catch on and you'll find her fitting the bowls together and taking them apart with ease.

If you are using measuring cups for this activity, start by giving your baby only three cups (one cup, 1/2 cup, and 1/4 cup). When she has mastered putting these together, you can give her a new challenge by adding the 1/3 cup and 2/3 cup. ✱

17. FIXING DINNER

Age Range
15-18 months

Materials
- Foods
- Playdough
- Kitchen utensils

Your baby is at an age when he loves to imitate what you do — and he's probably getting quite good at it. His desire to imitate you helps him learn many new skills. So encourage him!

When you're together in the kitchen you may notice your baby imitating your actions. Take advantage of his interest and let him help you while you enjoy the pleasure of each other's company. If you're fixing a salad, your baby can help you tear the lettuce. You can also begin to encourage good health habits by helping him wash his hands before handling the food. Seat him at a table and give him a large bowl and a leaf of lettuce. Show him how to hold the lettuce in one hand over the bowl and how to tear off small pieces with his other hand. Sit next to your baby as you prepare vegetables for the salad. Talk to him as you work and let him know how much you appreciate his help.

Your baby can also "help" you make gelatin, a cake, or anything else that needs stirring. Give him a spoon and a bowl. Pour a little of the mixture into his bowl **and let him stir to his heart's content. If he** needs help, you can place your hand over his as he holds the spoon. Move your hand in a stirring motion. When your baby is stirring a liquid, be sure the bowl isn't very full in order to avoid spills. If you don't want any spills, put a few dried beans or some rice in a bowl for your baby to stir. He can also stir pieces of playdough.

At times your baby may want to help you but because of the type of food you are preparing, it may not be practical. You can still give your baby a chance to imitate what you are doing by giving him playdough to use. (A recipe for making playdough appears in *Educating on a Shoestring*.) Store the playdough in a can with a plastic lid, such as a coffee or shortening can, so it will not dry out. If you keep it in your kitchen, it will always be handy when your baby decides he would like to help the chef.

If you are making hamburgers, you can roll the playdough into a ball and show your baby how to flatten it with the palm of his hand. Give him a spatula and let him try to flip the "hamburger" (or "pancake"). Or give your baby a large piece of playdough to tear into smaller pieces. Use your imagination and suggest a variety of playdough dishes for your baby to prepare.

18.   SETTING THE TABLE

Age Range
15-18 months

Materials
• Napkins
• Silverware

If kitchen chores are getting you down and you could use a helping hand, this activity is designed for you. You may find there is a willing helper right under your nose — don't let the diapers fool you. With a little practice you may soon find that your baby's help is invaluable.

By including your baby in the task of setting the table you are giving her an opportunity to imitate you. There will be a limit as to what your baby can do. You obviously won't want to ask her to put anything on the table that is heavy, sharp, or breakable. But she can put a napkin by a plate.

Talk to your baby as you show her how to place a napkin by each plate. **"We need to put a napkin by each plate. First, I will put a napkin by Daddy's plate. Next, I will put a napkin by Joey's plate. Now I am placing a napkin by Mommy's plate. You need a napkin. Can you put a napkin by your plate?"** Hand your baby a napkin. If she doesn't seem to know what to do, give her some help: **"That napkin goes by your plate. Let's put it there."** Walk over to your baby's plate and help her put the napkin next to it. **"Good, now every plate has a napkin next to it. Thanks for helping me."**

Continue to give your baby the opportunity to practice placing a napkin by her plate when you set the table for other meals. When she can do this with ease, ask her to place a napkin by each of the other plates. Walk around the table with her. Stop at each plate, hand her a napkin, and ask her to place the napkin by the plate. As she catches on, you will no longer need to walk around the table with her. Give her a napkin and tell her whose plate to put it next to.

Once your baby masters napkins, she can move on to silverware. Give her one piece of silverware and tell her whose plate to place it next to. At this point in your baby's table-setting career, you can't be too picky about which side of the plate the silverware goes on. As long as each person has a set of silverware within arm's reach, your baby deserves a vote of thanks.

Chore-time Chums

1. Looking at Lights
2. Looking and Listening
3. Cradle Gym
4. Looking Up
5. Turning Toward the Source of a Sound
6. The Playpen
7. Exercising in a Jumper Seat
8. Sitting Alone
9. Moving Toward a Toy
10. Peek-a-Boo
11. Looking at Myself
12. Hide-and-Seek with Objects
13. Recognizing Sounds
14. Playing Catch
15. Crawling Through a Tunnel
16. Matching Socks
17. Dusting
18. Putting Away Toys

1. LOOKING AT LIGHTS

Age Range
Birth-3 months

Materials
• Strand of twinkle lights that give off very little heat

Young babies enjoy looking at lights. Even a newborn will stare intently in the direction of a lamp or sunny window. For variety, use a strand of twinkle lights (commonly used to decorate Christmas trees) to entertain your baby while you clean a room.

Put the string of lights where the baby can see them easily. If he* is a newborn (birth-1 month) place them to his side, since newborns usually lie with their heads turned to the side rather than straight ahead. You might drape them along the side of his crib or hang them from a nearby doorknob. If the baby is a little older, sit him in an infant seat. He can look at the lights as they hang across an opened drawer or as they lie wound together in a ball of light on a table.

While you dust or vacuum, jiggle the strand of lights occasionally and talk to your baby about what he sees: **"Look at these pretty lights. They're sparkling white. We hang them on our tree at Christmastime."**

2. LOOKING AND LISTENING

Age Range
Birth-3 months

Materials
• Laundry to be folded

You don't have to entertain your newborn constantly, but she* enjoys your company immensely and learns a great deal from the words and caresses you offer her. Even a task as ordinary as folding laundry can become an entertaining adventure in learning.

Folding laundry.

Place your unfolded laundry on a sofa or bed, and lay the baby next to the laundry pile. As you fold each item, hold it up for her to see. Wave the item slightly and describe it: **"This is your brother's shirt. What pretty stripes it has — red, green, and brown."** If possible, fold the clothing while you hold it up so that the baby can see what you're doing. Occasionally rub an item gently against her cheek so she can feel its texture.

---

*In odd-numbered activities, the baby is referred to as a boy. In even-numbered activities, the baby is referred to as a girl.

---

*In even-numbered activities, the baby is referred to as a girl. In odd-numbered activities, the baby is referred to as a boy.

You might also sing this song to your baby as you work, using the tune to "Here We Go 'Round the Mulberry Bush":

This is the way we fold our clothes,
Fold our clothes, fold our clothes.
This is the way we fold our clothes,
Early in the morning. 🧍

3. CRADLE GYM

Age Range
Birth-3 months

Materials
• Homemade cradle gym (see below)

Once your baby starts to become aware of the world around him, he will begin to reach out with his hands to touch things that he sees. During the second month he'll begin to wave his arm in the direction of attractive objects, and by the third month he'll be able to hit his target fairly often and pat it with his fist. During these weeks, mobiles and cradle gyms are especially fascinating to your baby. He can look at them, touch them, watch them move, and listen to the sounds they produce. You can make a very simple cradle gym for your infant that will entertain him for short periods of time while you do household chores.

Stretch a heavy string across the baby's crib and tie it tightly to the two upper bars. Then cut several short pieces of elastic (about 8" long). Securely tape the end of each elastic piece to a small lightweight object, such as a ball of crumpled paper, a small stuffed animal, or a ribbon tied in a bow. Noise-making objects are especially attractive to a baby — for example, a jingle bell (larger than 1" diameter), a rattle, or a securely sealed plastic medicine bottle containing a dried bean. Tie the free end of each elastic piece to the piece of string that

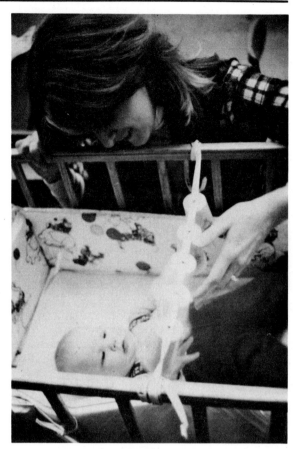

A variety of crib toys is available in stores.

is stretched across the crib. The objects should hang about 6" above the mattress.

Lay your baby in his crib so that the suspended objects hang above his tummy. If he doesn't notice the objects, tap them lightly so that they move. Your baby will enjoy looking at them and touching them. Although at this age he is not yet able to grab and hold on to objects, he will enjoy batting the hanging trinkets with his fist. Change the objects every few days so that your little one will have new things to examine. If he seems content, leave him alone with his toy for 10 or 15 minutes while you squeeze in a waiting chore. Once your baby can grab objects on his own, do not leave him alone with a homemade gym that has tape or other small objects that he might put in his mouth and choke on. 🧍

4. LOOKING UP

Age Range
3-6 months

Materials
• Laundry to be folded

By this time your baby should be able to hold her head up at a 90° angle when you place her on her tummy. She'll enjoy looking around while she's in this position, at least for short periods of time. When you are sorting and folding laundry, you can play a looking game with your baby as she lies on her stomach.

Put a pile of clean laundry on the floor and place the baby nearby on her tummy so that she's facing you. As you remove each piece of clothing from the pile and fold it, talk to her: **"Look at this pretty shirt. It's your mommy's favorite one."**

Whenever you select a brightly colored item from the pile, use it to play a brief looking game. Stand over the baby's head out of her sight. Then lower the laundry item until it's in front of her face. Jiggle the item so that she watches it intently. Then slowly raise the piece of laundry and talk to the baby so that she looks up to see it: **"Look up. The shirt is over your head now."** If she sees your grinning face above her head, she may wiggle her body in excitement and do some "swimming" with her arms and legs.

Then drop the piece of laundry in front of your baby so that she can reach for it and examine it while you sort and fold other articles from the laundry pile.

5. TURNING TOWARD THE SOURCE OF A SOUND

Age Range
3-6 months

Materials
• Noisemaker

Your baby is quickly becoming more mobile. Although he is not yet crawling, he can twist his body in order to see all around him. By six months he can probably turn over from front to back *and* from back to front. You can take advantage of his increasing mobility to play a listening game while you dust and clean a room.

Lay your baby faceup on the floor in the middle of a room that you plan to dust. Carry a bell or other noisemaker with you while you clean the room. As you work, ring the bell and talk to your baby: **"(Baby's name), listen to the bell. It's over here."** He should then turn in the direction of the sound. If he doesn't, move within his view while you make the sound.* When he does look toward you, praise him and give a big smile: **"You found me. I have the bell!"** Move around the room and ring the noisemaker as you clean. From time to time, walk over to your baby and give him a kiss and a hug. Then ring the bell over his head and let him reach for it.

Turn your baby over and try this activity while he is lying on his tummy. He may even manage to pivot his body around in order to see you.

---

*If your baby consistently fails to turn toward the noisemaker, be sure to have his hearing checked.

6. THE PLAYPEN

Age Range
3-6 months

Materials
- Playpen
- 4 favorite toys

A playpen can be a special place for your baby to learn and explore on her own. Some people feel that a playpen is like a little jail where a baby is unstimulated and miserable. This is true if you put your baby in a playpen too often or for too long a time. But well-planned playpen time can give your baby the necessary opportunity to play by herself for about 15 minutes while you do a household job. A good playpen also acts as a "safety zone," protecting the baby when you have to leave the room for a short time.

Help your baby feel at home in the playpen.

If you do plan to use a playpen, it's best to introduce it to your baby at this age so that she can become accustomed to it early on. Place about four very attractive toys in the playpen for your baby to enjoy. If you stock it with too many things, she will be overwhelmed and confused. Talk to her and show her the toys so that she feels relaxed and happy: **"See the funny clown that I put in with you. She's smiling!"**

Some babies enjoy the playpen more if a person is in the room with them. Others play better in the playpen when no one is around. Experiment with your own baby. Then set up the playpen so that she is either near you or alone, depending on which she prefers. While your baby is playing you can concentrate on your work. But check back periodically to see whether she is still enjoying herself in the playpen.

7. EXERCISING IN A JUMPER SEAT

Age Range
6-9 months

Materials
• Jumper seat
• Toy and string, paper bag, flashlight, radio or record player

Your baby may enjoy bouncing in a jumper seat. Jumper seats come in two styles: a seat that hangs from a doorway by a spring, and a chair set in a frame with springs. Both can let your baby feel independently active, and both provide a good way for him to exercise his legs and arms and coordinate large muscles. While you are cleaning a room in your house, put the jumper seat in a spot where your baby can see you. He will enjoy his time in the jumper seat much more if he can watch you while he plays by himself.

When you put your baby in the seat, make sure that his feet touch the floor. Then bounce him up and down a few times. Talk to him enthusiastically while you bounce him until he begins to push with his feet: **"Up and down. Look at you go! Push with your feet."** Then while you work in a

nearby area, your baby might jump and bounce, turn the seat around with one foot, look down and watch his feet, or "talk" to you happily.

You can also add some attractions to his bouncing area to make jumping time more fun:

• Suspend a toy by a piece of string so that it hangs next to your baby in his seat. Make sure it hangs above his head so that his neck won't become entangled in it. He can hit it and make the toy twirl, or grab it and play with the toy as he bounces.

• Place a large paper bag on the floor in front of your baby's seat. Put something heavy in the bag to anchor it in place. Your baby will enjoy grabbing the bag and rustling the heavy paper.

• Shine a light from behind your baby's seat so that his body casts a shadow on the floor. He can watch his shadow "dance" as he jumps.

• Turn on the radio or play a record. Clap and dance to the music for a while as your baby bounces. When you return to your work, he may continue his dance. ✳

8. SITTING ALONE

Age Range
6-9 months

Materials
• Familiar playthings

Your baby's ability to sit alone depends on the development of her muscles and spine. If you think she might be strong enough to sit without props, put her in a sitting position and then let go cautiously. If she

Dancing and exercising.

105

slumps forward or falls to the side, wait a week or so and try again. When she does sit alone, she will use her arms to prop herself up. Eventually she'll be able to sit with her arms free. Then you can play a game to help her strengthen the muscles she uses for sitting.

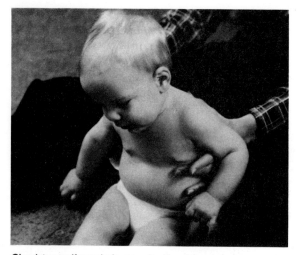
Check to see if your baby can sit without your help.

While you are cleaning a room, seat your baby on the floor and surround her with toys. As long as she is interested in the playthings you can get some chores done. Carry a few extra playthings with you in a pocket. From time to time, approach your baby from behind and get her attention with one of the toys: **"Look what I have for you — it's a mouse that squeaks. Turn around and get it."** Your baby should turn while sitting and take the toy from you. Praise her after she grasps the plaything: **"You turned without losing your balance!"**

To make the game more fun, offer the toy from one side one time and from the other side the next time. When she turns, hand her the toy with a hug. When she can sit very steadily, hold the toy over her head so that she has to reach up to get it. 🧒

9. MOVING TOWARD A TOY

Age Range
6-9 months

Materials
• Favorite playthings

Before your baby actually crawls on his hands and knees, he will probably develop some way of scooting around. He may roll from one place to another, pull himself with his arms, or flip-flop his body in his own way. While you are doing housework, you can encourage your baby to move himself toward several enticing toys.

Before you clean a room, gather some of your baby's favorite toys. Then place him on his tummy in the room where you will be working. Place one of the toys in front of him, just beyond his reach. Talk to your baby and encourage him to move toward the toy: **"Here's your car. Come and get it."** If he has trouble moving and becomes frustrated, move the toy closer so that he can reach it with his outstretched arm. When he grabs the toy, praise him and let him play with it for a while as you clean.

Moving toward a noisy rattle.

After your baby becomes tired of the toy, hold another one in front of him. Encourage him to wiggle toward it and grab it. Before you finish cleaning the room, your baby might scoot toward quite a few toys. ✶

10.   PEEK-A-BOO

Age Range
9-12 months

Materials
• Towel, blanket, or newspaper

Playing peek-a-boo will usually get a few smiles and giggles from your baby. It will also teach her that things exist even when they are out of sight. You can play a game of peek-a-boo anytime there is a towel, blanket, or newspaper handy. So if your baby is in the bathroom with you while you are changing towels, seat her on the floor, grab a towel, and have some fun.

Tell your baby that you are going to play peek-a-boo. Place the towel over your head. Wait a few seconds and then ask your baby, **"Where am I? Where did I go?"** Pull the towel off and say, **"Peek-a-boo! Here I am!"**

Then give your baby a turn. **"Now it's your turn."** Place the towel on her head. Wait a few seconds. Then remove it and say, **"Peek-a-boo! I see you!"**

As you play peek-a-boo, your baby may find this version of the game too easy. She'll let you know when she's ready for the more difficult version by trying to take the towel off herself. Take her hand and help her pull the towel. You can also encourage her to take the towel off your head in the same way. Don't forget to say "Peek-a-boo!" each time she removes the towel. ✶

11. LOOKING AT MYSELF

Age Range
9-12 months

Materials
• Full-length mirror
• Toy, cracker, hats

When you notice your baby pinching his stomach or carefully examining his hands, he is learning about someone very important — himself. He is learning that he is the one who is moving those fingers and that the big round thing he sees when he looks down is part of him as well. In order for your baby to learn about all the parts that make him the person he is, he must see (and feel) them. An activity as simple as looking in a mirror is a great way for your baby to develop self-awareness. Next time you have to do some mending or letter writing, move to a room where there is a full-length mirror and take your baby along.

Looking in a mirror.

Seat your baby in front of the mirror and let him explore his image. He may reach out and touch that "other person" he sees or babble to the person in the mirror for a while. Give him a toy so he can see himself move his hands as he plays. Eating a cracker in front of a mirror can also be very enlightening. As your baby eats he will see his mouth, tongue, and teeth. Try putting a few old hats on the floor next to your baby. Show him how to put one of the hats on his head. If he catches on, he may put the hats on and take them off by himself. If so, he may play peek-a-boo with himself.

When you are finished with your chore or if you just need a break, join your baby in front of the mirror. What could be more exciting to him than seeing you in duplicate? ✶

12. HIDE-AND-SEEK WITH OBJECTS

Age Range
9-12 months

Materials
• Favorite toy

Remember those days when you could take something from your baby without a fuss? As far as your baby was concerned, if she couldn't see the object, it no longer existed. But as your baby gets older, she is also getting wiser. It may not be as easy, now, to rescue your shoes from her grip and hide them somewhere. Chances are, those shoes will find their way back into her hands. When you are rescuing your shoes for the second time, remind yourself that by finding an object you have hidden, your baby is solving a problem. She is also learning that objects continue to exist even when they are out of sight.

There are good hiding places in just about every room in your home. So when you find yourself working and your baby is nearby, take time out for a game of hide-and-seek. Sit on the floor with your baby near a hiding place such as a chair, couch, plant, or bookshelf. Show her a toy and ask her to hold it: **"I have your toy**

puppy. You hold the puppy." Let your baby hold the toy for a few seconds. Then take it from her and hide it while she is watching you: **"Where did the puppy go? Can you find it?"** Your baby may go straight to the hiding place and squeal in delight at having found the puppy.

If your baby needs help, have the puppy peek out from its hiding place: **"Where did the puppy go? There he is. He's hiding behind the chair."** If she still isn't sure where the puppy is, guide her hand to the hiding place. **"There's the puppy. You found him."** Once your baby catches on to the game of hide-and-seek, use other objects and hiding places. Play the game as long as she is interested and having fun.

13. RECOGNIZING SOUNDS

Age Range
12-15 months

Materials
- None

Your baby has been surrounded by sounds since birth. (In fact, there is evidence that the fetus can hear sounds as early as the fourth month.) Now that he's celebrated his first birthday, he is ready to begin connecting sounds with the things that make them. He probably has already shown you that he associates certain sounds with their source. For example, the sound of keys opening a door may send him scrambling to greet a loved one. Take time out from your busy day to share some sounds with your baby. When you do, he will be developing his listening skills as well as learning more about the world around him.

Recognizing a dog's barking.

As you clean, you will be making a lot of sounds to which you can call your baby's attention — the vacuum cleaner, a broom sweeping across a floor, water running. You may also hear a clock ticking, the telephone ringing, a dog barking, and music playing. When you hear a sound, get your baby's attention: **"Listen, (baby's name). Do you hear that?"** Listen together for a moment. Then tell your baby what is making the sound and, if possible, show him where the sound is coming from by pointing: **"I hear some children laughing outside."**

As long as there is a sound to hear, you can play this game with your baby. If things get unusually quiet, you can always make a few noises yourself by knocking on a door or whistling. Don't limit the game to noises you hear while at home. Also point out sounds you hear while outdoors, shopping, or in a restaurant. When you notice your baby stopping an activity to listen to a sound, take the opportunity to tell him what is making the sound. 🧍

14. PLAYING CATCH

Age Range
12-15 months

Materials
• Socks

Your baby will need a lot of practice before being able to play a game of catch with you. A good time to give her some practice is while you're folding laundry. You will also be giving yourself a break and sharing some special moments with her. Don't worry if you don't have a ball handy. All you need for this impromptu game of catch is a pair of socks rolled into a ball.

When you're with your baby and feel like a game of catch, grab two socks from the laundry basket and make a sock ball. Then sit opposite her on the floor and roll the ball to her. Chances are, your baby will find the ball intriguing and will pick it up. If she doesn't, encourage her to do so by saying, **"Pick up the ball, (baby's name)."**

If your baby picks up the ball, show her how pleased you are by saying, **"That's right, you picked up the ball."** Then hold out your hands and ask her to throw the ball back to you. She may find it more interesting to chew on the ball than to throw it. If so, encourage her by tapping on the floor or by clapping your hands. Be sure to ask her again to throw the ball to you. The ball is likely to land just about anywhere during your baby's first attempts at throwing. Praise any effort she makes, even if she only drops the ball.

If your baby doesn't drop or throw the ball, show her what to do by gently pushing it out of her hands. Then roll it back to her. Once again, ask her to throw it to you. If she still doesn't attempt to drop or throw the ball, she may not be ready for a game of catch. Let her play with the sock ball her own way. Wait a week or two and then try the game again. 🧍

15. CRAWLING THROUGH A TUNNEL

Age Range
12-15 months

Materials
• Sheet
• 2 chairs

As your baby moves freely around your house, he will begin to learn about the size of various spaces in relation to his own size. He may already have discovered that crawling under the dining room table is a breeze, but getting under the end table is a different story. You may have to "rescue" him because he has become stuck trying to crawl through the legs of a chair. Your baby learns from these experiences. To give him additional practice, use a sheet to create a "tunnel."

Crawling through a cardboard-box tunnel.

Drape the sheet over two chairs to form a tunnel. Put your baby in front of one end. Move around to the other end so he can see you when he looks through the tunnel. Encourage him to crawl through: **"Come to Grandpa. Come and get me."** If your baby seems hesitant, crawl partway into the tunnel and then encourage him to come to you once more. You can also try crawling through the tunnel starting from his end. Encourage him to crawl after you. An older brother or sister may enjoy crawling through the tunnel with the baby on his or her heels.

Your baby may think the tunnel is fine for you to crawl through, but he may prefer to take a path around it to get to the other end. If so, he still deserves a hug for his effort. Try making a sheet tunnel again in several weeks. By then he may be ready to take the direct route from one end to the other.

16. MATCHING SOCKS

Age Range
15-18 months

Materials
• 2 pairs of socks of different colors
• Clothing items

When your baby was younger she may have "helped" you with the laundry by pulling all the clothing out of the laundry basket. She may now be ready for an activity that's more challenging and a bit more helpful — matching socks.

Place two socks of different colors (for example, white and black) in front of your baby as you say, **"Can you help Daddy with the laundry?"** Hold up the mate to one of the socks: **"Here is a white sock. Where's the same sock? Can you put it with the white sock?"** Hand the sock to your baby so she can put it with the other white sock. Then hand her the black sock: **"Where is the same sock? Can you put it with the other black sock?"** It will be a while before she learns the names of the colors, but matching by color is a step toward that goal.

You can also teach your baby to put big socks together and little socks together. Say, **"Look, this sock is big. It is Daddy's sock. Can you find another big sock?"** When she finds a big sock, let her know how pleased you are with her accomplishment: **"You did it! You found a big sock. It is big, just like this one."**

Also try placing one of your baby's shirts in front of her and asking her to find another shirt that belongs to her. Or show her an article of clothing that belongs to you and ask her to find something else that you wear. Your baby can learn more than matching skills when you include her in laundry-day chores. She can learn the names of colors and of clothing. She can learn the words *big*, *little*, and *same*. You can also teach her the word *soft* by letting her feel a flannel nightgown and the word *rough* by feeling a pair of corduroy pants. The chore of doing laundry can become a pleasure when you turn your basket of laundry into a basket of learning. ✘

17. DUSTING

Age Range
15-18 months

Materials
• Old white sock
• Felt pen

Life for your baby so far has been a challenge — and he has proved that he doesn't shy away from challenges. If he did, he wouldn't have learned how to sit up, crawl, stand, walk, or feed himself. It is important to recognize your baby's limits, but it is equally important to challenge him. Helping you with the dusting may just be the new challenge your baby needs. He won't see it as work but as another opportunity to imitate you. To add to his fun, make a puppet out of an old white sock. Near the toe, draw a face with a felt pen. We've named this puppet "Duster."

Next time you dust, introduce Duster to your baby. Slip your hand into the sock and talk for Duster: **"Hi, (baby's name). I'm Duster. My name is Duster because I like to wipe the dust off furniture. Let me show you how I dust."** Select a piece of furniture to dust. It should be low enough for your baby to reach; for example, a coffee table, a low shelf on a bookcase, or the legs of a chair. If there are breakable items on the furniture, remove them before dusting. If you are dusting a chair, show your baby how Duster wraps himself around the top of the chair leg and slides down.

Next, select a piece of furniture for your baby to dust. Remove any objects that are on top of the furniture. Put Duster onto your baby's hand and then guide it across the furniture several times. Then let him try it by himself: **"Now you dust all by yourself."** Grab a dustcloth and work alongside him dusting the same piece of furniture or one nearby. If he stays interested, send him and Duster to another piece of furniture. Whether your baby plays or dusts with Duster, bring the sock out only when you are dusting or are doing other household chores. This way Duster will remain special. ✘

18. PUTTING AWAY TOYS

Age Range
15-18 months

Materials
• Toy box, plastic laundry basket, or decorated cardboard box

Just as diapers and bottles go with babies, so do toys. When it comes time to put away your baby's toys for the day, it may seem as if they have multiplied. Rather than putting the job off until your baby is tucked into bed, select a time when she can help you. Working with your baby will make the job more enjoyable for you, and she will be learning to follow directions and to help herself.

Keep a toy container in the room in which your baby usually plays. She has probably seen you put her toys away many times. But make a point of having her watch you put several of her toys into the box after she is finished playing. Talk with your baby as you are putting the toys away: **"I am putting your favorite truck into the toy box. You had a lot of fun playing with it today, didn't you? Now I am putting the big red ball away."**

After your baby has watched you for a week or two, ask her to help. When there are four toys left, hand one to her and pick up one for yourself. **"I'm going to put the bear into the toy box. Now you put the bell you are holding into the box."** If your baby doesn't seem to understand, help her put it away. Hand her another toy and take the last toy yourself. **"Now I am putting the doll into the box. You put the block into the box. There, that job is done. All the toys are put away. Thank you for helping me."**

Eventually you'll be able to sit back and watch your baby put away toys.

Ask your baby to help you whenever it is time to put toys away. After she has mastered the job of putting two toys away, ask her to join you when there are more than four toys left. For each toy you put away, ask her to put away one. Also try leaving the last two toys for her to put away by herself. In your own way, always let your baby know how much you appreciate her help. 🧒

Bathtime Business

1. Bending and Stretching
2. A Little Conversation
3. Enjoying the Water
4. Lying in the Tub
5. Enjoying a Back Massage
6. Water Toys
7. Picking Up and Dropping
8. Knocking Down a Tower
9. Playing with Water
10. Bathtime Potpourri
11. Putting Things into a Container
12. Uncovering a Hidden Toy
13. Learning to Follow Directions
14. Washing Hands
15. Blowing Bubbles
16. Selecting an Object
17. Pointing to Body Parts
18. Getting Undressed

1. BENDING AND STRETCHING

Age Range
Birth-3 months

Materials
• Towel

Even a newborn can benefit from simple exercises that strengthen muscles and help make him* aware of his body. Bathtime is a good time to do such exercises because he is relaxed and free of constricting clothing. Any firm surface will make an excellent exercise mat — a changing table, a firm mattress, or a floor covered with a clean towel.

After your baby is bathed and dry, place him on the firm exercise surface. (You may want to diaper him.) He should be lying faceup with his feet toward you. Take hold of each foot. Then gently move his legs in a circle as if he were riding a bicycle backwards. Make about six circles. Talk to your baby as he exercises and tell him what he's doing: **"You're making big circles with your legs. Round and round they go."** Then let go of his feet and gently run your thumb up his tummy toward his chest. He will tighten his stomach muscles **in response.**

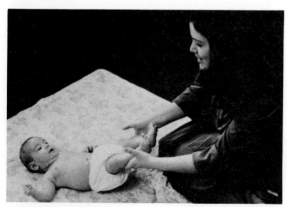

A little postbath exercise.

*In odd-numbered activities, the baby is referred to as a boy. In even-numbered activities, the baby is referred to as a girl.

Next, hold the baby's hands. Make sure that he's limp and relaxed. Slowly place his arms down along his sides and then up over his head. Then hold them out at right angles to his body. Finally, if he is enjoying the exercises, cross his arms over his chest and bring them down along his sides again.

Do not exercise your baby for more than five minutes at a time or he will become overly tired. After you finish, give him a kiss and tell him what a good job he did.

2. A LITTLE CONVERSATION

Age Range
Birth-3 months

Materials
• None

Bathtime can be fun for you and your baby. Even a fussy baby will usually relax in the bath and take a calm look at the world around her.* Take this opportunity to have a "conversation" with your little one.

As you wash your baby, talk about each body part and describe what you are doing: **"Now I'm washing your hand. Your fingers are curled up tight. Open your fist so I can wash your tiny fingers."** Of course, she won't understand a word that you're saying. But she will enjoy listening to your voice and watching your face as you talk. By the third month, she will coo back to you. She will be especially delighted if you imitate her verbal sounds. The two of you might then carry on a lengthy conversation of "coos."

While drying the baby, kiss different body parts and tell her what you are doing: **"I**

*In even-numbered activities, the baby is referred to as a girl. In odd-numbered activities, the baby is referred to as a boy.

kissed your tummy. Now I'll kiss your elbow." She will wiggle and grin during this game.

3. ENJOYING THE WATER

Age Range
Birth-3 months

Materials
- None

As your infant enters his third month, he will probably turn bathtime into splashing time. Because he feels comfortable in the water and is free from clothing, he uses this opportunity to kick and wave his arms and wiggle all over. The following activity can add a new dimension to his bathtime during the third month.

Fill your bathtub until the water level is about 6". Then hold your baby faceup in a horizontal position. Support him under the neck and shoulders with one hand and under his bottom with your other hand. Lower him into the bathtub while you hold him in this manner. Then glide him back and forth in the water as you talk to him: **"Look at you. You're floating in the water. You look like a real swimmer."**

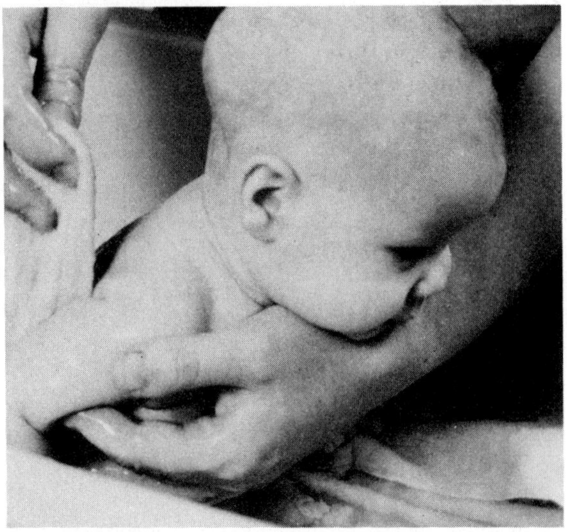

Scrub-a-dub-dub!

If your infant enjoys the water, he will kick and squirm and grin at you. But if he cries in alarm, take him out and comfort him. Then try this water activity another time. After your baby has finished his bathtub swim, give him his normal bath.

4. LYING IN THE TUB

Age Range
3-6 months

Materials
• Towel

If your baby is a water lover, she will shower you with splashes during bathtime as she kicks and waves her arms. Before she is able to turn over from back to front, try this bathtub activity.

Fill your bathtub until the water is about 1" deep. Then lay your baby faceup in the tub. If you think she might try to turn onto her side, prop up her head with a folded towel. In any case, hold your hand near her head in order to keep her from turning it into the water. After you place her in the water she may be quiet and puzzled with her freedom. Once she feels confident, she will move her arms and legs and wiggle her body with excitement.

With your free hand, pour water from a cup onto your baby's tummy, feet, or hands. **"Here comes the water. Now there's a waterfall coming down on you."** Before your baby becomes too tired, remove her from the tub and snuggle her in a warm towel. ✤

5. ENJOYING A BACK MASSAGE

Age Range
3-6 months

Materials
• Blanket
• Baby lotion (optional)

You can end bathtime in a special way by giving your baby a back massage. As he becomes accustomed to massages, you might also use this way to calm him when he is upset or to put him to sleep if he is overtired and fussy.

Before you dress your baby after a bath, lay him on his tummy. You might put him on a blanket on the floor and kneel next to him. Or you can sit down and lay him across your knees. Make sure your hands are warm before you begin — no one can enjoy an icy massage! You might put lotion on your hands and rub them together briskly to make them feel warmer.

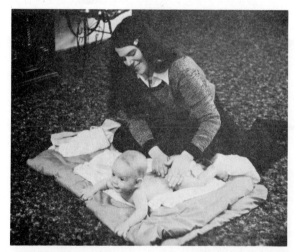

Many babies love to be massaged after a bath.

Place your hands next to each other on your baby's neck. Then slowly move them to the left and the right as you massage down to his bottom. Then move your hands in the same way back up to his neck. Talk to your baby soothingly: **"Nice and slow. I bet that feels good."** The massage may relax your baby and put him to sleep, or it may invigorate him so that he kicks and waves his arms in delight. ✤

6. WATER TOYS

Age Range
3-6 months

Materials
• Tub toys (see below)

Over the next few years the collection of toys in your bathroom will grow and change. Water adds a special quality to toys, and even at this young age your baby can enjoy playing with them in the tub. Any waterproof household items can serve as water toys — plastic containers, funnels, Ping-Pong balls, empty shampoo bottles, washcloths, plastic straws.

Fill your baby's bath until the water is waist deep on her. Place a toy in the water and seat her in the tub. While you support her in a sitting position with one hand, tap the toy and draw her attention to it: **"Look at this bottle. It's floating right to you."** Hold the toy above the water and drop it. **"Smack! That made a loud noise."**

Swish your hand in the water so that the toy moves around. Then help your baby touch the toy with her hand: **"Get that toy, (baby's name). It's escaping!"** Don't expect your baby to grab the toy while it's in the water, but with practice she'll be able to touch the floating toy with her hand while you hold her in a sitting position. 🧍

7. PICKING UP AND DROPPING

Age Range
6-9 months

Materials
• Tub toys

Now your baby can easily pick up objects within his reach, but letting go is not always as easy. To give him practice at bathtime, challenge him to pick up toys that are bobbing in the water and to let go of them to make a little splash.

Seat your baby in a shallow bath — about 2″ deep. He should be able to sit by himself, but be prepared to catch him if he slips and falls over. Drop several plastic toys into the tub and act delighted when they splash: **"Oh! What a splash. Your boat is in the water."** Move the floating toys in your baby's direction. He may have trouble when he tries to grab a toy. If so, place his hand around the bobbing toy so that he can lift it out of the water.

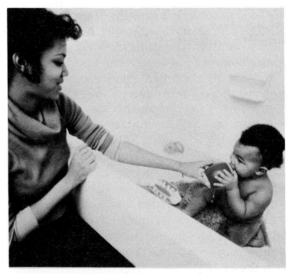

Getting ready for some football in the tub.

After your baby has had a chance to examine the toy for a while, encourage him to drop it. Demonstrate with other toys:

"Look at this ball fall into the water. Splash! Drop your toy, too." If your baby does not let go of his toy, demonstrate again. Offer lots of praise when he lets go, even if he did so accidentally. It may take many tries before your baby can *deliberately* drop a toy and make it splash. ✻

8. KNOCKING DOWN A TOWER

Age Range
6-9 months

Materials
- Plastic containers
- Towel or rubber mat (optional)

Once your baby sits up alone, bathtime can become even more of a learning adventure. If you do not have appliques on the bottom of your tub, seat your baby on a towel or rubber mat so that she won't slip and fall. Always stay close to her when she's in the tub and be ready to catch her if she loses her balance. When your baby is in the water, you can play a game of "Topple the Tower" with some plastic food-storage containers.

Fill your tub until the water is about 2" deep. Gather several plastic containers with lids; tall, narrow containers work best since they topple easily. Fill one container with water and use it for the bottom of your tower. Then while your baby is sitting, build a tower with three or more containers. **"Look at this tall tower. There are four containers in it: one, two, three, four."** Knock the tower over and congratulate yourself: **"Yeah! I knocked over the tower. What a splash!"**

Build the tower again. This time wait for your baby to knock it over. If she doesn't, take her hand and help her. Laugh and praise her after the tower falls: **"You did it too! You knocked over the tower!"** Rebuild

Play "Topple the Tower" after bathtime, too.

the tower and encourage your baby to knock it down each time. Eventually she will topple the tower without your help. ✻

9. PLAYING WITH WATER

Age Range
6-9 months

Materials
- Tub toys

Water can be endlessly entertaining to your baby. At bathtime you can amaze him by just filling the tub. He can watch the water as it pours from the faucet, listen to the sounds it makes, and feel it rush into the bathtub. Before using this activity, make sure that your water heater is set no higher than 120° F. If you can't control the heat, have a plumber install a mixing valve to protect your baby from scalding-hot water.

Before you fill the tub, undress your baby for his bath. Then turn on the faucet and close the drain. Keep the water pressure low so that the tub fills slowly. When the water temperature is comfortable, seat your baby in the tub and let him watch the water rush from the faucet. Hold his hand under the running water. If he tries to grab the column of water, he will be surprised to see it splash over his fist.

Put some toys in the tub under the running water. Your baby can watch them bob up and down. Help him pick up a floating toy and hold it under the faucet. The water will splash off the toy in all directions. Talk to him about the water: **"Oh! The water is spraying on your tummy. Does it tickle?"** When the water reaches bathing level, turn off the faucet and give your baby his regular bath.

10. BATHTIME POTPOURRI

Age Range
9-12 months

Materials
• Sponge, washcloth, Ping-Pong ball, spoon, cup

Once your baby can sit up steadily in the tub, bathtime will become a whole new adventure for her and you. There will be more space to move around in and more water to splash. Be sure to put a mat in the tub so she won't slip as she explores during bathtime. Since you are with your baby during her bath anyway, roll up your sleeves and join in the bathtime fun. Try some of the following activities.

• Show your baby how to hit the water with the palm of her hand to make a splash.

• Give her a sponge to squeeze.

• Pour water over her hands.

• Put only an inch of water into the tub. Let your baby lie on her stomach and on her back.

• Let her feel the washcloth when it is dry and then when it is wet.

• Push a Ping-Pong ball under the water. Let go of it so it will pop up.

• Drop something heavy into the water, such as a spoon. Encourage your baby to pick it up off the bottom of the tub.

• Give her a cup. Show her how to fill it with water and how to pour the water out.

• Play a game of peek-a-boo using the shower curtain, if you have one.

11. PUTTING THINGS INTO A CONTAINER

Age Range
9-12 months

Materials
- Gallon-size cardboard milk carton or plastic bowl
- Ping-Pong balls, corks, plastic animals, fishing bobbers, or small tub toys (larger than 1" diameter)

You can turn bathtime into a learning experience by letting your baby drop objects into a container while he's in the tub. Dropping objects into a container gives your baby practice at grasping and releasing. This activity is also good for developing eye-hand coordination.

For this activity you will need a "boat" and some "cargo." To make the boat, cut off the bottom half of a gallon-size cardboard milk carton. If you don't have a milk carton, you can use a plastic bowl. The cargo must float and be small enough to fit into the boat.

Place the boat in the water in front of your baby, saying, **"I've made a boat for you to play with."** Let him play with the boat for a few minutes. Then place the cargo in front of your baby: **"Here are some corks. Watch me. I'm going to put the corks into the boat."** Pick up a cork and drop it as you say the word *in*. Drop the other corks into the boat, one at a time.

Take the corks for a short ride in the boat. **"The corks are in the boat, (baby's name). Now you put a cork in the boat."** Dump the corks out of the boat so they are in front of your baby. Ask him to pick up one of them and put it in the boat. The objects may be a bit difficult to pick up since they will bob in the water. If he is having trouble getting hold of one, pick it up for him. Then ask him to take the cork from your hand. If he hesitates, put the cork in his hand. Hold the boat under your baby's hand and ask him to drop the cork into the boat. If he doesn't let go of the cork, loosen his grip. **"Look! The cork is in the boat. You dropped the cork into the boat."** Take the cork for a short ride and then come back for another one if your baby is enjoying the game.

Play the game each bathtime until your baby can put all the cargo into the boat. At first he may put only one object into the boat. But with time he will be able to fill the boat with three, four, or more objects. To keep the game interesting, change the cargo every few days. ✳

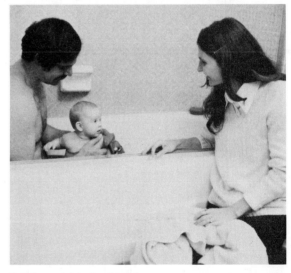

Bathtime can be a family affair.

123

12. UNCOVERING A HIDDEN TOY

Age Range
9-12 months

Materials
- Washcloth
- Floating toy small enough to fit under washcloth (but larger than 1" diameter)

If your baby thinks the only purpose of bathtime is for her to have fun, this activity should fit in well with her bathtime games. If she isn't too keen on bathtime, the activity may help her change her mind. Besides being fun, it will help your child learn to solve problems and learn that objects still exist even when they are out of sight.

When your baby is in the tub, show her the toy and let her hold it for a few minutes. Then take it from her and place it in the water in front of her. Cover the toy with the washcloth and ask, **"Where is the toy? Where did it go?"** Remove the washcloth and say, **"Oh, here it is. It was hiding under the washcloth."**

Play the game several more times, encouraging your baby to lift the washcloth off the toy. If she doesn't join in the fun, you may need to give her a peek at the toy or take her hand and help her lift the washcloth. If she still isn't interested in playing, try the game again in several weeks or try it on "dry land" with a toy that may be more appealing to her. ✘

13. LEARNING TO FOLLOW DIRECTIONS

Age Range
12-15 months

Materials
- Bathtub items whose names the baby knows

By now your baby may have several words in his vocabulary. Once he has learned the names of some objects, he can begin to follow simple directions. At the same time that he's learning to follow directions, you may find that his ability to hear you seems to vary greatly. He may hear you perfectly when you ask him to hand you his shoe, but when you ask him not to play with the knobs on the TV, his hearing may suddenly seem impaired. Your baby is showing you through his behavior that he is beginning to understand the implications of his actions. By now he probably has a good understanding of the word *no*.

Prepare your baby's bath as you normally would. While doing the activity you are going to ask your baby to hand you several objects. It is important that he is familiar with the names of the objects you are using. They should also be things that interest him. If he usually plays with a boat and washcloth during bathtime, they would be good items to use for the activity.

Put a washcloth in front of your baby and say, **"This is a washcloth."** Hold out your hand as you say, **"Give me the washcloth."** If he doesn't seem to understand, place the washcloth in his hand. Then guide his hand so he gives you the washcloth. **"You gave me the washcloth. Thank you."** Place another item in front of your baby and ask him to hand it to you.

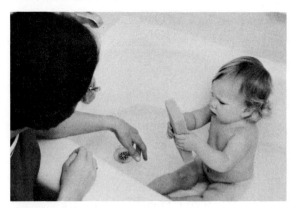

Your baby may not want to hand over an interesting item like a sponge.

Also try playing this game at the end of your baby's bath. Ask him to hand you his bath toys one at a time. As he hands something to you, put it on the side of the tub in a bucket or wherever you store the toys. You can also play this game as you dress your baby. When it is time to put on his sock, shoe, or coat, place it in front of him and ask him to hand it to you. Through this activity your baby will also be learning new words. 🧒

14. WASHING HANDS

Age Range
12-15 months

Materials
• Soap

It will be a while before your baby can give herself a bath. But you can introduce her to the task by teaching her how to wash her hands at bathtime. By learning this skill, she is one step closer to being able to care for herself.

When your baby is in the tub, show her how to dunk her hands in the water to get them wet. If she doesn't seem to understand, hold her wrists and dip her hands into the water: **"I'm putting your hands in the water. Now they're all wet."** Turn one of her hands palm side up and then rub the bar of soap over the palm: **"I'm putting soap on your hand."** Take your baby's other hand by the wrist and rub her hands together: **"Look, (baby's name). You're washing your hands."** Let go of her wrists to see if she will rub her hands together by herself. You can rub *your* hands together as an example for her. While you both rub your hands, sing the following song:

> *This is the way we wash our hands,*
> *Wash our hands, wash our hands.*
> *This is the way we wash our hands,*
> *So they will be all clean.*

Show your baby how to put her hands into the water to rinse them off. **"Now it's time to rinse off the soap. Put your hands into the water and swish them around."**

Let your baby wash her hands each time you give her a bath. Encourage her to do as many steps as she can by herself — getting her hands wet, rubbing her palms together, rinsing the soap off. If your baby isn't always sure what to do, show her and encourage her to imitate you. Praise her while she is washing and after she is finished: **"You did such a good job of washing your hands. They're so clean."** You may even want to call in another family member so your baby has a larger audience to watch her latest accomplishment. 🧒

15. BLOWING BUBBLES

Age Range
12-15 months

Materials
- Bubble-blowing liquid
- Plastic wand

Bubbles are fascinating and fun. *Blowing* bubbles is a good activity for a child who is learning to talk, because it encourages him to control his breathing. The bathtub is an ideal place to blow bubbles when you are inside, since you never know where a bubble will land and leave a wet reminder of its existence. Bubble liquid can be made by mixing some dish detergent with water.

Demonstrate how to blow a bubble.

First, show your baby how to blow: **"Watch me blow."** Blow into your baby's hand so he can feel the air. Then show him how to blow into the wand to make bubbles. Hold the wand in front of your baby's mouth and encourage him to blow. It may take him a while to get the hang of blowing. No, or little, air may come out during his first attempts. If the activity is too difficult, try it again when he is a little older. But don't put the bubbles away. Your baby will still enjoy watching *you* blow. He may even try to pop any bubbles that come his way (which is good practice for coordinating his eye and hand movements).

Make sure that the bubble-blowing liquid is not poured into the tub. The liquid contains detergent that's harsh on the baby's skin. It can cause dryness or a rash, and in little girls it can lead to irritation of the urethra and infection of the urinary tract.

126

16. SELECTING AN OBJECT

Age Range
15-18 months

Materials
- Bathtub items: toys, washcloth, soap, bowl, cup, ball, plastic bottle
- Cookie sheet (optional)

Your baby understands many more words than she is able to say. She may even understand more words than you give her credit for! To get an idea of what words she does know, try the following activity while giving your baby her bath. As you do the activity she may learn some new words.

Place three objects in front of your baby. You can use her bath toys, a washcloth, or a bar of soap. You can also gather some extra objects. Choose things that are waterproof and familiar to your baby. (You can use a greater variety of objects if you set them on a cookie sheet. Since the cookie sheet floats, it will protect the objects from the water.)

Once you have set three objects in front of your baby, ask her to pick up one of them. Start with the thing you think she knows the best. She may know the word but hesitate because she doesn't understand your directions. If she seems confused, help her pick up the object: **"That's right, (baby's name). You picked up the duck."** Put the duck down and ask your baby to pick up something else. If she hands you the wrong thing, take it from her and put it down. Say again, **"Pick up the soap."** Put your baby's hand on the soap and help her pick it up: **"Good job. You picked up the soap."** Put the soap down and ask her to pick it up once again. As you continue to play the game, vary the objects you use.

You can play this game at other times — when you have a few minutes to sit down on the floor or when you're getting her dressed. The more you play the game, the more opportunity your baby has to learn new words and to master old ones. ✖

17. POINTING TO BODY PARTS

Age Range
15-18 months

Materials
- None

Watching your baby grow and learn is one of the joys of being a parent. Nothing can replace the feeling you had the first time your baby repeated "mama" or "dada" after you. Your baby will be learning new words throughout his life. But you have the privilege of teaching your baby to understand and to say many of his first words. Learning the names of body parts is especially meaningful for your baby because he is not only learning new words but also learning more about himself. Bathtime is a good time to teach him the names of body parts since he can see all of them undisguised by clothing.

Your baby will probably attach meaning to a word before he can actually say it. He'll be able to point to a dog before he'll be able to say "dog." When teaching your baby the names of body parts, begin with any body part you like, but teach him the names of only one or two at a time so he won't be confused. For example, take his hand and touch his leg: **"This is your leg. You are touching your leg."** Then wash your baby's leg, talking to him as you do so: **"I'm washing your leg with soap. Now I'm rinsing your leg. Your leg is clean now."** Take your baby's hand again and have him touch his leg. Do the same for his other leg. Then wash his other leg and touch and name it again.

After you have done this for several days, begin the activity by saying, **"I'm going to wash your leg. Where is your leg?"** Your baby may point to his leg as if he's known all along where his leg was. If your baby still isn't quite sure what a leg is, take his hand and place it on his leg: **"That's your leg."** Ask your baby once again where his leg is and see if he'll touch it without your help.

As your baby learns to point to the parts of his body, you can play a game as you wash him. Tell him what part of his body you want to wash and ask him to show you where it is: **"I want to wash your arm. Where is your arm? That's right. That is your arm."**

As you do this activity, your baby will hear you name the parts of his body many times. He may surprise you sometime and repeat the name after you. Act delighted and ask him to name the body part again: **"What is this? That's right. It is your arm."** Encourage your baby to name other body parts by asking, "What is this?" as you or he points to it. ✶

18. GETTING UNDRESSED

Age Range
15-18 months

Materials
• None

Since your baby has to get undressed before each bath, it is a natural time to teach her how to undress herself. At this age there is a limit to how much you can expect her to do. Teaching her to undress will be a step-by-step process that will take many months. It may seem like extra work for you now, but when the day comes that your baby undresses herself, it will all be worth it. The independence your child gains by being able to undress herself will help you and will make her feel grown up.

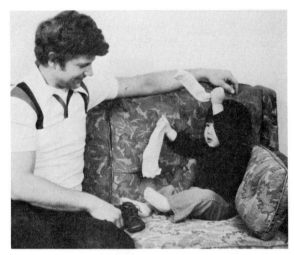

Step one: removing socks.

Socks are probably the easiest piece of clothing to take off, so let your baby begin with them. Pull her sock away from her toes so she can get hold of it easily: **"Pull your sock off, (baby's name). Pull."** Show her what you mean by tugging at her sock. She may have trouble getting the sock over her heel. If so, slip the sock past her heel and then ask her to pull it off the rest of the way.

Your baby can also help you by lifting her arms when you take off her shirt. Raise your arms up and ask her to do the same: **"Lift your arms up like me."** At first you may have to lift them up for her. Another way to get her arms up is to play a game of "How Big Is Baby?" When she lifts her arms as you say "So big!" remove her shirt.

Your baby can also help as you take off her pants by lifting up her leg. Tap on one of her legs and ask her to lift it. If she is not sure what to do, put your hand behind a knee and lift the leg up for her. Let your baby hold on to your shoulder so she won't lose her balance. ✶

Shop, Look, and Listen

1. Looking Around at the Store
2. Discovering Animals
3. The Check-out Counter
4. Stop and Go
5. Playing in the Stroller
6. Examining Objects
7. Entertaining in the Car
8. A Trip to a Fabric Shop
9. A Trip to a Music Store
10. Grocery-Store Games
11. Smelling Spree
12. Sharing Food
13. A Trip to a Hardware Store
14. Eating in a Restaurant
15. Sidewalk Safety

1. LOOKING AROUND AT THE STORE

Age Range
Birth-3 months

Materials
• None

During your baby's first month, the stimulation of a shopping trip might be too much for him* to handle. But don't worry. Whatever a newborn can't handle, he will simply shut out. That's why he will probably sleep through a trip to the store and then wake up the moment you return home. But after a few weeks your baby will enjoy looking around in stores and listening to all the sounds.

Wait until your baby is awake and alert before you do your shopping. A tired infant is a cranky infant. While you shop you might carry the baby in an infant carrier or hold him in your arms. As you walk through the store, look at him from time to time. If he is staring at something in particular, stop and let him watch for a short while. Talk to him as he looks: **"That's a bright blue light. It turns on and off so fast. Isn't it pretty?"** If you notice something attractive, especially moving objects, hold your baby facing it so that he can take a good look. He might like to look at jewelry cases, lighted displays, popcorn popping in a machine, and active children.

Don't be surprised if the excitement wears out your baby. He will probably fall asleep sometime during your walk through the store. 🧍

2. DISCOVERING ANIMALS

Age Range
3-6 months

Materials
• Animals in a pet store

If you have time to spare when you are shopping in a mall or a department store, introduce your baby to the pet department. Many large stores sell pet birds and fish as well as pet supplies. The bright colors and quick movements of these animals will fascinate your baby.

If there are fish in the pet department, hold your baby fairly close to the tank. She* will be especially attracted to brightly colored fish such as goldfish or neon tetras. She will also enjoy the shiny gravel in the tank and the bubbles created by the motorized water filter. Talk about whatever catches her eye: **"Those fish are swimming back and forth. That pink gravel is pretty!"**

Parakeets and other birds will delight your baby. They are beautifully colored, and they move from perch to perch quickly. They also make exciting chirps and other noises. As you watch the birds, imitate some of their noises for your baby and talk about them: **"The bird is drinking water from his dish. Now he's sitting on the swing. Look at him go back and forth."** BE SURE TO KEEP YOUR BABY'S FINGERS AWAY FROM THE CAGE. Birds nip little fingers. 🧍

---

*In odd-numbered activities, the baby is referred to as a boy. In even-numbered activities, the baby is referred to as a girl.

*In even-numbered activities, the baby is referred to as a girl. In odd-numbered activities, the baby is referred to as a boy.

3. THE CHECK-OUT COUNTER

Age Range
3-6 months

Materials
• None

Shopping trips are filled with sights and sounds for your baby to learn from. One stop on your trip that's sure to fascinate him is the cash register. Whether the register is a standard electric one or the more modern, computerized kind, your baby will enjoy the noises and movements that the machine produces and the busy activity of the clerk behind the counter.

During many of your shopping trips, you'll be too busy to try this activity. But at times when both of you are relaxed, you can make check-out time a new adventure. As you approach the register, lift your baby out of his infant stroller or the shopping cart. If you have to wait in line, talk to your baby about the things he notices: **"Look at those red gloves. Would you like to touch them?"**

As the clerk rings up your items, hold your baby close to the register so that it grabs his attention. He may cause you to notice movements and sounds that you usually pay little attention to, such as lights on the register, the noise produced when the keys are pressed, the surprise of the register drawer popping open, the clinking of coins, and the crinkling of the shopping bag. ✗

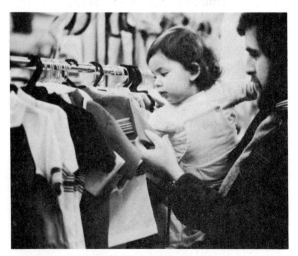
An older baby can help choose clothing.

4. STOP AND GO

Age Range
6-9 months

Materials
• None

Before your baby begins to talk, she will learn the meanings of many words. The next time you're shopping in a grocery store, play a game to help her understand the words *stop* and *go*.

Place your baby in the child's seat of the grocery cart. If she needs support, prop her up with a coat or diaper bag. Begin to push the cart and say to your baby, **"Here we go. Go, go, go!"** As you walk along, talk to her about what you need to buy and what you are looking for. Then as you stop to put something into the cart, say, **"Now we're going to stop. Stop. Stop!"**

Continue this game as you move up and down the aisles. Don't be afraid to act like a ham — your baby will love it. You might say the words *stop* and *go* in a sing-song voice or tilt your head from side to side as you speak. You might also stop and start the cart several times in one aisle (as you say "stop" and "go") without actually looking for food items. But if you do, your baby may protest when you do interrupt the game to put something into the cart! ✘

5. PLAYING IN THE STROLLER

Age Range
6-9 months

Materials
• Shoelace
• Favorite toys

Although your baby enjoys the sights and sounds in a store, he may not always be on best behavior when you are shopping. Just when you're searching for a particularly hard-to-find item, he may decide that it's time to be carried or entertained. By attaching a toy to his stroller or carrier, you can delay some of his fussiness.

Before you leave your house, put several toys in your baby's diaper bag. When you are at the store, use a shoelace to tie a toy securely to your baby's stroller or carrier in a place where he can easily reach it. Then while you walk around the store, your baby can enjoy the toy.

After a while, attach a different toy to the stroller or carrier and continue your shopping. From time to time change the toy again. Your baby will remain content for a longer time if you change his plaything often. ✘

6. EXAMINING OBJECTS

Age Range
6-9 months

Materials
• Items in grocery store

Think of all the time you spend at the grocery store. More than a little, so make the most of it! At this age your baby enjoys the commotion in a busy store. As you walk up and down the aisles you can help her investigate the things in this intriguing place.

Seat your baby in the child's seat of the shopping cart, propping her up if necessary with a coat or purse. As you shop, involve your baby as much as possible. Tell her the name of each item you choose. Then before you put it into the cart, help her inspect it. Shake the item for her to see if it makes a sound. If the item is lightweight and unbreakable, let her hold it and examine it carefully. Otherwise, put her hand on the item so she can feel it. If it's a refrigerated food, tell her that it's cold. Describe any other obvious characteristics:

- **"This potato is hard."**
- **"Look at this big watermelon."**
- **"This grapefruit is round."**

If the item has a strong smell, hold it near your baby's nose. You might let her sniff an onion, an orange, coffee, soap, or a spice such as cinnamon.

Examining fruit.

7. ENTERTAINING IN THE CAR

Age Range
9-12 months

Materials

- Pinwheel
- Car seat

When you go shopping with your baby there is lots to do and see once you reach your destination. At the store there are people for him to watch and lots of interesting things for him to look at. But the trip there and back can be a bit dull at times. One way to entertain your baby while riding in the car is to attach a pinwheel to the back of the front seat of the car. While your baby sits safely strapped into his car seat in the back seat, he can watch the pinwheel spin.* This is most entertaining, of course, during nice weather when you have the car windows down so the air can blow the pinwheel.

Pinwheels are very inexpensive and can be purchased at many discount stores, dime stores, toy stores, and drug stores. Show your baby the pinwheel before attaching it in the car. Blow on it so that it moves: **"This is a pinwheel. See how pretty it looks when it moves."** Then tape the pinwheel to the car seat so it will spin to the incoming breeze. To be sure it will catch the breeze as the car moves, you may need to position it while someone else is driving. To make sure it stays in place, put the pinwheel out of your baby's reach. Don't let your baby play with the pinwheel. It has tiny, sharp parts.

You can stress the word *stop* when the car and pinwheel stop and the word *go* when

*Make sure that your baby is always strapped into a properly installed, federally approved car seat. Leaving your baby loose in the car or in an inadequately secured car seat is the most dangerous thing you can do. Make every ride a safe ride.

the car and pinwheel go: **"We are going to stop now. Look, the pinwheel stopped also. Here we go again. The pinwheel is going, too."** ⚉

8. A TRIP TO A FABRIC SHOP

Age Range
9-12 months

Materials
• Fabrics

You don't have to be a seamstress or tailor to enjoy looking in a fabric shop. Fabric comes in an array of glorious colors, eye-catching patterns, and interesting textures. The cloth is fun to look at and to feel. A tour of a fabric shop is also a good learning experience for your baby. During one of your shopping trips together, take time out to look through a fabric shop. Since part of the fun of being in a fabric shop is feeling the textures of the cloth, be sure you have a baby with clean hands.

As you walk past the fabric, select one or two things to point out to your baby. Perhaps the fabric is a striking color: **"Look at this pretty red cloth. Here is another piece of red cloth. It is red, just like your shirt."** Or you may see a piece of cloth with a pattern in it that is familiar to your baby: **"Look. There are little yellow ducks on this fabric. The ducks look just like the duck you play with at bathtime. Ducks go quack, quack, quack."** Let her feel some of the fabric as you talk about it — *soft, bumpy, tickly, rough*. You can also point out shapes in the fabric: **"There are circles on this fabric. And this fabric has squares on it."** Trace around the shape with your finger.

Continue the tour as long as your baby stays interested. ⚉

Toddling down an aisle — with some help.

9. A TRIP TO A MUSIC STORE

Age Range
9-12 months

Materials
• Musical instruments
• Homemade instruments (see below)

Many shopping centers contain at least one musical-instrument shop. Next time you're shopping, stop into one of these stores and let your baby enjoy the wonderful sounds created by the variety of musical instruments.

Select several different instruments to show your baby, such as an organ or piano, a guitar, and a flute. Before starting the tour, explain to the salesperson what you are doing. He or she may be willing to play the different instruments for your baby. If not, ask if it is all right for you to hit a note or two on the piano and strum the guitar. Chances are, there will be demonstration models on the floor just for this purpose. As you are showing your baby an instrument, repeat its name several times. You can also stress words such as *big* (piano), *little* (harmonica), *loud*, and *soft*. Continue the tour as long as he is interested.

few beans can become a maraca. You can further develop your baby's awareness of music by playing records or turning on the radio. Of course, if you play an instrument, give your baby a special performance from time to time. Or if you have any musical friends, ask them to play for your baby when you visit them. ✖

A young toddler will "tell" you when it's time to go shopping.

Musical instruments are very appealing to children, so your baby may want to try to make beautiful sounds just as you have. When you get home, you can offer him some homemade instruments to experiment with. Two pan lids can become cymbals; a wooden spoon and an empty oatmeal box can become a drum; and an empty potato-chip cylinder containing a

10. GROCERY-STORE GAMES

Age Range
12-15 months

Materials
• Items in grocery store

One of the stores your baby is most familiar with is probably the grocery store. It's full of many different things, so it's a good place for her to learn new words. Since many of the things at the grocery store are also in your home, you can work on the words in both places. Hearing the names of things over and over in a variety of places will help your baby to remember them.

Since every grocery store has a freezer section, it is a good place to introduce the word *cold*. Let your baby touch a frozen orange-juice can or a carton of ice cream: **"This ice cream feels cold. Brrr. It is cold."** Let your baby touch something else cold: **"This package of corn is also cold. Touch it. It feels cold."**

You can also introduce your baby to the words *big* and *little*. Show her a pair of similar objects that are very different in size. For example, you might hold up a 6-ounce jar of pickles and a gallon jar of pickles. Then label them as *big* and *little:* **"Here is a big jar. It's so big! This one is little. Big . . . little."** 🧍

11. SMELLING SPREE

Age Range
12-15 months

Materials
• Fragrant items found in stores

Your baby has several ways to become acquainted with and identify items. He can identify things by sight, touch, sound, and taste. He is also able to identify some things by the way they smell. During an upcoming shopping trip, plan to give your baby's sense of smell a workout. In fact, both of you can enjoy the fragrances of many of the items found in stores.

When passing a cosmetics counter, stop to let your baby smell some of the perfume or scented soap. If possible, include a florist shop on your "smelling spree." There are often enticing fragrances coming from restaurants, bakeries, and popcorn stands. Call your baby's attention to each of the smells. Tell him what it is he is smelling: **"I smell popcorn. It sure smells good."** Or: **"Smell this flower. It looks pretty and smells sweet. I like to smell flowers."** Grocery stores are also full of good things to smell. Let your baby smell some of the items before you put them in the cart. Fruit, spices, and bread are all nice to smell.

Calling your baby's attention to the smells around him may help him become more aware of them as he grows older. And it gives him a treat now. 🧍

12. SHARING FOOD

Age Range
12-15 months

Materials
• Nutritious snack

It is often a good idea to have a nutritious snack in the middle of a shopping trip. Besides filling an empty spot in your stomach, it gives you a chance to rest and to talk about the things you have seen and the things you are going to do. You can enjoy two tastes by buying a small treat for your baby and one for yourself and then sharing them. Plan the snack so it won't spoil your baby's appetite for her next meal.

Snack time at the grocery store.

Divide your baby's snack into small bites as you normally would. After she has sampled the treat, ask her to give you a bite: **"That looks good. May I have a bite of pretzel?"** If your baby isn't sure what you want her to do, place a bite in her hand and guide it to your mouth: **"Mmm. That's very good. Thank you for sharing. Now you take a bite."** After she has eaten a few more bites of her snack, offer her a bite of yours: **"I'd like to share my yogurt with you. Take a taste."** Ask your baby to share her snack with you again.

Play this game at home during a meal or snack. Your baby will probably be delighted to feed the grown-up who usually feeds her. After playing the game awhile, you may find her offering you food uninvited. Use this activity at other times to encourage your baby to try new foods.

13. A TRIP TO A HARDWARE STORE

Age Range
15-18 months

Materials
• Items in hardware store

Next time you need to pick something up at the hardware store, take your baby and take a look around. There will be lots of new things for him to see, and some familiar things as well. Name some of the items you see and talk about how they are used.

As you walk through the paint department, let your baby feel the bristles on a paintbrush. Tickle his nose with the brush. Show him a *big* paintbrush and then a *little* one. Pretend to paint something with the brush. Point out pretty colors on the paint color chart. Name the colors he is most familiar with, such as red, blue, and yellow.

Show your baby a nail, a screw, and a hook as you walk through the hardware department. Hardware comes in all sorts of interesting shapes. Pick out a few of the more unusual things to show him. You can show him how a washer is round and how a nut screws onto a bolt. Let him feel a spring and squeeze a piece of rubber tube.

While at the hardware store you can also help your baby understand simple opposites. Each time you take an item out of its container, stress the word *out*. Stress the word *in* each time you put it back: **"I am taking the screw out of the bucket. Now I am putting it in the bucket."** See if your baby understands the words by asking him to take something out and to put it back in. If he isn't familiar with the name of the item, you may have to point to show him what you're talking about.

Try snacking *before* you leave home.

As you go past something your baby is familiar with, stop and ask him if he sees the item: **"I see a sponge. Do you see a sponge? Where is it? Point to the sponge."** He may enjoy showing you how much he knows by pointing out familiar things.

14.   EATING IN A RESTAURANT

Age Range
15-18 months

Materials
• Bib, soda crackers, child-size spoon and cup, washcloth, toys (all optional)

Eating out occasionally can be a pleasant treat for the whole family. There is no food to prepare, no dishes to wash. It also gives you a chance to eat food you don't normally have at home. The experience will help your baby become familiar with one more aspect of the "outside world." She will see that eating a meal in a restaurant is different from eating at home. It's likely your baby will enjoy the change as much as you do.

A little planning can help assure that dining out will be an enjoyable, relaxing time for everyone. Try to select a restaurant that caters to families. They will be used to serving children and more likely to accommodate any special needs or requests you have. In many family restaurants you get a bib and soda crackers along with the high chair. But if this is your first trip to the restaurant with your baby, take these things along just in case. The crackers may be a big help if it takes a while to receive your food. You may also want to take along a child-size spoon and cup and a damp washcloth in a plastic bag. It never hurts to bring a few small toys as well.

When you get a menu, show it to your baby. Explain that it tells you what things they have to eat. Name a few of the items: **"They have fish, orange juice, and green beans here. Those are all things you like to eat."** When the waiter comes, let your baby know that you are ordering food for her: **"(Baby's name), I am ordering some soup, a grilled cheese sandwich, and a glass of lemonade for you."**

If the restaurant kitchen is accessible, show your child where the cooks are preparing the food: **"See, they are cooking your sandwich on that grill."** While everyone is eating, expect your child to stay in her seat and eat her meal. Do not linger and chat for a long time after everyone is finished — your child will only get restless and cranky.

When it's time to go, explain to your baby that you must pay for the food: **"Now we**

have to give the cashier some money for the food we ate." Let your baby watch as you pay.

15. SIDEWALK SAFETY

Age Range
15-18 months

Materials
- None

On a nice day, you and your baby can get some fresh air and exercise by walking to a nearby store. You may visit an ice-cream shop, a refreshment stand in a nearby park, or even a gas station. The purpose of this activity is to introduce your baby to safety habits while walking outdoors. It will be a while, of course, before he will be able to walk any distance on his own. But when that day comes, you can have some peace of mind knowing that he is aware of the "rules of the road."

Point out to your baby that each time you come to a corner you must stop: **"We are at a corner so we must stop. Now we need to look down the street to see if there are any cars coming. Do you see a car? No. Now we look down this way for cars. There are no cars there either, so we can go. Take my hand so we can cross the street."** Repeat this procedure each time you come to a corner and must cross a street.

Point out stop signs to your baby: **"That sign says 'Stop.' It is telling the cars that they must stop."** If you come to a stoplight, tell your baby that red means *stop* and green means *go:* **"The red light is on, so we're supposed to stop. Now the light is green, so we can go."**

You can play a "Stop and Go" game as you are walking, to help your baby understand what the words mean. Hold your baby's hand. Tell him that everytime you say "Stop," you are going to stop walking and when you say "Go," you will start to walk again. Say "Stop" and "Go" several times during your journey.

Teaching — Family Style

1. Mealtime
2. Dancing with the Family
3. Smiling at Faces
4. Enjoying Others
5. Shaking a Rattle
6. Exercising Legs
7. Feeding Myself
8. Stopping a Ball and Picking It Up
9. Looking at a Book
10. Watching a Puppet Show
11. Follow the Leader
12. Retrieving Bean Bags
13. Batting a Balloon
14. Family Song Time
15. Building with Blocks
16. Naming Family Members in Photographs
17. Pantomiming
18. Pop Goes the Weasel

1. MEALTIME

Age Range
Birth-3 months

Materials
• None

Meals are a time of day when the whole family can be together. And this includes your infant. Although he* is not yet ready to eat with the "big people," he can join the family and make his own special contribution.

When you set the table for a meal, leave a space for the baby's infant seat. If there is no room on the table, put the infant seat on the floor in a spot where he can see everyone.

While the family is eating, ask them to show the baby any eating utensils and brightly colored foods that will attract his attention. Remind them to turn to him occasionally and ask questions: **"What do you think, (baby's name)? Can your brother bring a friend on our trip to the beach?"** Everyone will enjoy the baby's responses when he frowns, goes slightly cross-eyed, or gives a tiny coo. He may even bring a light note to a heated family discussion.

By including the baby as a regular family member, you have a chance to promote a feeling of togetherness and to help older siblings overcome jealous feelings they may have. You are also helping the baby become acquainted with his family in a pleasant way. ✶

---

*In odd-numbered activities, the baby is referred to as a boy. In even-numbered activities, the baby is referred to as a girl.

2. DANCING WITH THE FAMILY

Age Range
Birth-3 months

Materials
• Record player or radio

If you have other children, you've probably discovered that there are times when everyone wants to be entertained at once. Dancing is a wonderful way to amuse all ages at the same time. And if your baby is awake and alert, she* will enjoy a dancing session as much as the others.

Dancing with twins.

---

*In even-numbered activities, the baby is referred to as a girl. In odd-numbered activities, the baby is referred to as a boy.

Use an area of your home where there is room for movement and a source of music, such as a radio, stereo, or a child's record player. If possible, offer the older child or children several types of music to choose from. The choices might include folk music, classical music, popular tunes, religious songs, marches, or children's songs.

While the music is playing, hold the baby and dance around the room. Encourage the others to join you. Everyone might sing along as you dance, and the others might sing to the baby as she peeks over your shoulder.

Continue the session as long as everyone is having fun. If your baby becomes overwhelmed, she will let you know by falling asleep or crying.

3. SMILING AT FACES

Age Range
Birth-3 months

Materials
• None

Your baby's first smiles can be a delight for everyone. He is beginning to communicate his feelings *voluntarily,* and so he seems more and more like a little person to the people who see him every day. Try the following suggestions to make the baby's first smiling attempts into a special time for the whole family.

When your baby is awake and comfortable, talk to him and encourage a smile. Have other family members take a look. They will probably be eager to see him give a real smile. Then challenge each of them to inspire the baby's biggest grin. One person may make funny faces for the baby; someone else may kiss the baby's chin and

talk to him; another person may ring a bell and smile at the baby. Of course, some of these antics might scare the baby and bring on a frown or a cry. But then too, your baby is communicating his feelings to those around him. You can take this opportunity to emphasize to everyone that they should respect the baby's feelings.

An older brother can inspire a smile.

4. ENJOYING OTHERS

Age Range
3-6 months

Materials
• Lightweight object: colored paper, fabric, or napkin

If you have other children, they may be eager to play with their little brother or sister. Continue, though, to watch cautiously when they handle the baby and play with her. One game that will entertain your baby can be played with brothers and sisters of any age. If you have no other children, father, mother, grandparents, or anyone else might enjoy playing this simple game with the baby.

Lay your baby on her back on the floor. Tell the other children to watch as you wave the lightweight object over the baby's tummy until she notices it. Talk to her about the object: **"Look at this pretty red scarf. It has long fringe on the ends."** Then drop the object so that it lands on or near your baby's tummy. She may or may not look at it after it falls. Instead she will probably enjoy watching your happy face, and she might "talk" to you in return. However she responds, your little one will enjoy the attention and love you are showing her.

Let each of the children hold the lightweight object over the baby and drop it as you did. Remind them to aim for her tummy. Then challenge them to find other objects. Remind them that they must be *very* lightweight. Help preschoolers or younger children search for appropriate objects. Besides enjoying the baby's responses, your other children (even older ones) will be challenged by this game of "Search and Find." Assist young children as they drop their objects so that they will not get carried away and harm the baby.

5. SHAKING A RATTLE

Age Range
3-6 months

Materials
• Rattle
• Noisemakers: 2 pan lids, spoon and pan lid, sealed jar filled with beans or rice, plastic bowl and pencil, rubber band stretched around shoe box

Your baby's ability to grasp and hold objects will improve greatly over these three months. By the fifth month, he should be able to hold on to an object that you place in his hand. During the sixth month he will begin to reach for and grasp objects by himself. Once your baby can hold objects, he will enjoy shaking a rattle or other noisemaker to make sounds. In this activity he will be delighted to use his rattle to take part in a family rhythm band.

Provide an instrument for each family member. Put a rattle or other shake toy in the baby's hand. Then have the family play their instruments together. You might want to use a record or radio music to accompany the family band.

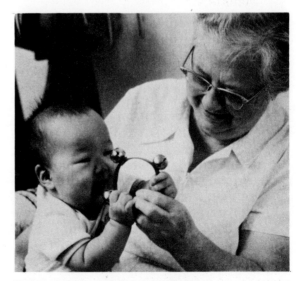

Shaking a rattle — with help from grandma.

145

Your baby will probably shake his rattle and wiggle his body in excitement as everyone plays. If he does not shake his rattle, hold his wrist and help him. If he drops the rattle, put it back in his hand so that he can continue to join in the fun. 🤸

6. EXERCISING LEGS

Age Range
3-6 months

Materials
• None

It will be several months before your baby is ready to walk. But she is already getting ready for that day. She kicks her legs vigorously and exercises them while lying on her back or in her infant seat. She may even dig her feet into the rug or carpet when she's on her tummy, as if to strengthen and coordinate her legs for crawling and walking. You can help your little one exercise her leg muscles as you sit and talk with family or friends, play a table game, or relax with the family and watch television.

Seat your baby on your lap so that she faces away from you. Hold her securely under her arms and lift her to her feet. Then simply let her push her feet into your lap as you hold her up. If she bends her knees and does not push, try the exercise again another time.

If your baby is facing another person or an attractive object, she will be more inclined to stretch her legs in excitement. She may also begin to push her feet if you bounce her up and down very gently. Do this exercise for only a minute or so the first time, and then gradually increase the amount of time. 🤸

7. FEEDING MYSELF

Age Range
6-9 months

Materials
• High chair
• Finger food

At mealtime your baby can join the family by sitting in a high chair that has a securely fitted tray. By now he is too active to sit safely in an infant seat. And he is now old enough to take part in mealtime with his own finger foods.

Put your baby in his high chair next to the table where the family is eating. Place some finger food on your baby's high-chair tray. Serve him small pieces of semi-soft food which he can swallow easily. He might like bread or toast, banana, cooked green beans or carrots, or pieces of boiled potato. Do not offer foods which need to be well chewed, such as nuts, popcorn, and raw vegetables.

While the family is enjoying the meal, encourage them to include the baby in the conversation: **"You're eating all by yourself, (baby's name). Does that taste**

Enjoying cereal bits and banana slices.

good? We're eating green beans, too. See, these are my green beans."

If your baby doesn't pick up his finger foods and eat them, place a piece of food in his hand. Then guide it toward his mouth and talk to him encouragingly: **"You can eat some banana. Good job! You put it in your mouth yourself."** The whole family should praise the baby whenever he does feed himself or even attempts to. Soon he will be showing off his eating skills to everyone. ✹

8. STOPPING A BALL AND PICKING IT UP

Age Range
6-9 months

Materials
• Tennis-size ball

Together with another family member you can teach your baby to stop a rolling ball and pick it up. When the weather is warm enough for your baby to sit in the grass, play this game outdoors. Play inside if the weather is cold or wet.

Sit in the grass with your legs spread apart. Seat your baby between your legs with her back against your lap. Then ask another member of the family to join you. Your game partner should sit with legs apart facing you and the baby. Hand your partner the ball and ask her or him to roll it toward the baby. Talk enthusiastically as the ball comes toward you: **"Here comes the ball. Catch it, (baby's name). Catch it!"** Place your baby's hand on the ball when it's within her reach. Praise her for stopping it: **"You caught the ball. Good catch!"**

Then throw the ball back to your game partner and play again. After a few times

see if your baby will try to stop the rolling ball by herself. Praise any attempts she makes, even if she just waves her hand in the direction of the ball.

Once your baby can stop the ball, encourage her to pick it up. Help her at first, and then after a few tries see if she will do it alone. Remember to praise her lavishly. Most likely, after she picks up the ball, she will bring it straight to her mouth. When she does this, pull it away gently and throw it back to your partner. ✹

9. LOOKING AT A BOOK

Age Range
6-9 months

Materials
• Storybooks with colorful pictures

Storybook time is a traditional favorite for all children. Even at this age your baby will probably enjoy a short picture book at bedtime. Older children, mom and dad, or other family members can look at a book together with the baby.

Use a picture book that has a single, colorful picture on each page. Even if your baby could focus on complicated pictures, he would become overwhelmed and lose interest in them quickly.

Sit with your baby on your lap and put the book on his lap. Let others sit next to you so that they can enjoy the book, too. As you look at each picture, ask the others to name it and tell your baby something about the pictured object: **"Tell the baby what that is. Tell (baby's name) about the bird. What color is it?"**

Let your baby touch each picture as you talk about it. Pull his head gently away from the book if he tries to bring the page

Try including an older child at story time.

to his mouth. Look at each picture for about 15 seconds — your baby's attention span is very short. Then let him touch the page as you turn it.

Look at one or two books regularly. Babies enjoy repetition — that's how they learn. Your baby will eventually become very familiar with the books and will enjoy recognizing the pictures and the sounds of their names. ✖

10. WATCHING A PUPPET SHOW

Age Range
9-12 months

Materials
• 2 puppets
• At least 4 blocks

Puppets always make good additions to your baby's collection of toys. She will enjoy them through her preschool years by changing the way she plays with them as she grows older. At this age, watching and participating in a puppet show gives her an opportunity to be a partner in play.

You will need two puppets for the following activity. If you prefer to make rather than buy the puppets, see *Educating on a Shoestring* for instructions.

Have two adults in your family be the first to present the puppet show. Or ask an older child to present it with an adult. If an older child is handling a puppet, practice the play a few times with her or him. The rest of the family can be the audience. Give the puppets names and introduce them to the audience. Have the puppets take turns talking with each person in the audience:

- **"What's your name? (Baby's name) is one of my favorite names."**
- **"I bet you are ticklish. Let me see."**
- **"You have cute pigtails. I like to pull pigtails."**

Once introductions are over, you can begin the puppet show. The following story involves Yippie and Yappie (substitute names of your choice). Set the blocks in front of Yippie, who will try to pick up one of them and set it on another.

YAPPIE: What are you doing, Yippie?

YIPPIE: I am *trying* to build a tower, but this block is too heavy. I can't pick it up!

YAPPIE: Maybe if I helped we could pick it up together.

YIPPIE: Thanks, Yappie. I sure could use your help. (Have the puppets struggle as if the block is heavy. After some effort they do manage to place it on top of another block.)

I can see this is going to be a big job. I have to put all these blocks on the tower and I'm already tired.

YAPPIE: I think we could use some more help. Could you help us, (baby's name)? Can you put this block on the tower? (Hand your baby a block and help her put it on the tower. If there are other people in the audience, give them a turn to put a block on the tower.)

YIPPIE: Thanks for your help. We never could have done it by ourselves.

YAPPIE: The tower looks great. It is so high. I've got to go now. Bye-bye.

YIPPIE: I've got to go, too. Bye. (Encourage your baby and the rest of the audience to wave good-bye to the puppets.)

Puppets foster language skills as well as entertain.

Create other simple plays. You can use stuffed animals and other toys as characters and props in your plays. Since your baby has a limited attention span, make the plays short. You can keep her interest by involving her in the plays. Have the puppets ask her to hand them things. If you have a "ticklish" puppet, your baby can take a turn at making the puppet laugh. Or she can put a handkerchief over the puppet's head for a game of peek-a-boo. If you have a puppet who likes to hide under bowls, in boxes, and behind books, your baby would probably be delighted to help another puppet find it. If you have other children, involve them in the plays. Older children may even enjoy making up some plays to present to the family. 🧑

11. FOLLOW THE LEADER

Age Range
9-12 months

Materials
• None

The time you spend together as a family will always be special, so plan some simple family activities in which your baby can take part. He's at an age when he enjoys imitating you, and he is getting quite good at it. "Follow the Leader" is a good imitation game for the whole family to play.

Decide which family member is going to be the leader. Everyone else should sit opposite the leader. You may want to seat your baby on your lap. The leader's job is to do a simple action that everyone else can imitate. As you imitate the action, encourage your baby to do so as well: **"Daddy is clapping his hands together. Mommy is clapping her hands together. And Jo Ellen is clapping her hands** together. **You clap** *your* **hands together."** If your baby doesn't join in, take his hands and clap them for him: **"That's right. You're clapping your hands together just like Daddy, Mommy, and Jo Ellen."**

The key to the success of this activity is that you do actions that your baby enjoys and can do. The following are a few ideas you can try:

- Cover your eyes with your hands, then remove them as you say "peek-a-boo"
- Cough
- Wave and say "bye-bye"
- Bounce up and down as you sit
- Rock back and forth as you sit
- Open and close your hand
- Make smacking noises as if giving someone a kiss
- Put your hand over your mouth
- Touch your foot
- Hit the floor with your hand

"Pat it and *roll it* and mark it with B."

12.   RETRIEVING BEAN BAGS

Age Range
9-12 months

Materials
- Bean bags
- Laundry basket

This activity makes use of the bean bags you made for your baby to touch and stack (see Activity 10 of *Just for the Two of You*). If you haven't tried that activity yet, see *Educating on a Shoestring* for instructions on making the bean bags.

Your family's part in this activity is to throw the bean bags into the basket. It can be an informal game of tossing, or each person can toss from a given distance and score a point for each basket she or he makes. Your baby's job is to take the bean bags out of the basket and give them to family members to throw. If she is standing well, she may be able to remove the bean bags from the basket without your help. (You may need to hold the basket so it doesn't tip over.) If she isn't standing yet, tip the basket so she can reach the bean bags. The person who is next in line to throw should encourage the baby to bring it to her or him: **"Bring Daddy the bean bag. Bring it here."** Your baby may decide to throw it rather than crawl over with it. After all, that's what everyone else is doing. Or she may just want to sit and hold the bean bag, or put it in the basket herself and then take it out again.

The direction the activity takes will depend on how many people are playing the game and how your baby decides she wants to participate. If only adults are playing with the baby, you can wait for her to take each bean bag out of the basket after you have thrown it. If there are other children playing, they may not want to wait. Supervise their throwing while the baby is near the basket. It's unlikely that a bean bag would hurt your baby if it hit her, but she wouldn't like it.

You may find it works best to have two baskets — one for the older children and one for grown-ups. However you play the game, your baby will be practicing skills such as crawling, throwing, taking an object from a container, and putting an object into a container. Most important, she will enjoy the feeling of being a part of the family. ✱

13. BATTING A BALLOON

Age Range
12-15 months

Materials
• Balloons

Many children find balloons fascinating. Perhaps it's because they are a bit unpredictable. They "float" in the air. They also let out a nice squeak when you rub your hand across them. And they never wander off too far, no matter how hard you hit them. Last but not least, they are inexpensive. While your children are young, always supervise them when they play with a balloon. If one should pop, throw it away immediately before it has a chance to make its way into your baby's mouth. Since playing with a balloon requires your supervision, it is a good activity to do as a family.

Batting at the balloon will give your baby practice coordinating his eye movements and arm movements. Chasing after it will give him a lot of practice crawling or walking. One of the greatest delights will be your baby's laughter as he plays.

You may need to show the baby how to bat the balloon. Place the balloon on the floor in front of him. Take his hand and show him how to hit the balloon. Then encourage him to go after it. Repeat this until he bats at the balloon by himself.

The whole family can join in the game. Have everyone get down on all fours. Your baby will enjoy having others down on his level for a change. Take turns batting the balloon, but let everyone chase after it once it is hit. And don't forget to include yourself in the game — join in the fun! ✱

14. FAMILY SONG TIME

Age Range
12-15 months

Materials
• Musical instruments (optional)
• Homemade instruments: 2 dowels, empty box, spoon and pot lid

There is nothing like an evening around the campfire singing your favorite tunes to the strum of a guitar. But even without the campfire and guitar, singing together can be great family fun. Listening to music and clapping along will help your baby develop a sense of rhythm. Clapping also helps her coordinate the movements of her muscles.

Give each family member a turn to choose a song to sing. Be sure to include some songs your baby knows well. Musical accompaniment is always an added pleasure — perhaps someone in your family plays an instrument, or you may have a recording of the song. But it certainly isn't necessary for a good time.

Get everyone into the act!

During some of your song fests, concentrate on clapping to the rhythm of the music. One member of your family should hold the baby on his or her lap so that the baby is facing the rest of the family. Clap your hands as you sing each song. Your baby may begin clapping her hands joyously. If she needs encouragement, take her hands in yours and clap them together. It will be a while before she can clap to the beat of music, but she can enjoy some plain old clapping for now.

Add variety to the songs by using homemade instruments. Beat out the rhythm of the songs by striking two dowel rods together. Or hit the top of an empty coffee can or oatmeal box with a stick or your hand. Hitting a spoon against a pot lid or shaking a bell adds a different sound to the band. It may take some practice getting everyone to play in time to the music, especially if you have other young children. Help your baby get acquainted with the instruments by taking her hands and helping her play. She will catch on with practice. If you find all this a little hard on the ears, limit the number of instruments that are played during each song. 🧍

15. BUILDING WITH BLOCKS

Age Range
12-15 months

Materials
• Blocks

Your baby will experiment with blocks before actually building with them. He may try to eat them or throw them. He may take them out of their container one by one and then put them back in the same way. To him, each block is just a colored cube. *You* can help him see that with a little imagination blocks can become trains, cars, houses, and boats. Get the whole family together to build a small city with blocks. Your baby will have an opportunity to play creatively with the rest of the family and to use his imagination.

While the other family members are busy building, take charge of the baby. Help him make things to add to the city. Show him how to stack two or three blocks to make a tower, or how to line up two or three blocks to make a train. Push the train along the floor as you add sound effects: *"Chug, chug. Whoo, whoo.* **Here comes the train."** With a push and a "vroom" one block can become a car. Try putting a few blocks in front of your baby to see if he'll try to build something. He may copy something you or another family member has built.

Encourage other family members to show the baby what they have built and to tell him about it. Your baby may think the demolition business is more fun than the building trade. This isn't a problem if other family members don't mind their creations being knocked down. But if they do, show your baby how to build his own tower to knock down, or build some for him. ✶

16. NAMING FAMILY MEMBERS IN PHOTOGRAPHS

Age Range
15-18 months

Materials
• Family photograph album

Looking through family photograph albums always brings back memories. Of course, your baby won't share in the memories but will still enjoy seeing pictures of herself and her family. This is a good time for her to practice saying the names of family members. Select an album that contains some recent pictures of family members and, if possible, that has only four pictures on each page. (The baby may have trouble paying attention if there are more than this.)

Sit so everyone is comfortable and can see the pictures. Your baby may enjoy sitting on your lap. When you come to a picture that is of someone your baby knows, ask her who it is. If she points at the person, say **"Yes. It's Mama."** Then take her finger and point it at the picture: **"Who is that?"** When your baby answers correctly, her mother can give her a big hug: **"That's right. It's Mama."**

Continue looking at the pictures as long as your baby is interested. Look at the photograph album regularly so she can continue to practice naming each person in the pictures. ✶

17. PANTOMIMING

Age Range
15-18 months

Materials
• Familiar objects: spoon, comb, cup, toothbrush, ball, plastic flower

Your baby may be ready to enjoy the fun of pantomiming. The act of pantomiming is challenging: when you show the child an object he must know what it is, understand how it is used, and then act out the way it is used. Although it's difficult, it is also a lot of fun, especially if the whole family joins in.

Pantomiming getting dressed.

Gather some objects your baby is familiar with. (You can also use pictures of objects, but this is a more difficult task.) Assign one person in your family the job of holding up the objects. He or she should sit opposite the other family members. As the leader holds up one of the objects, tell your baby what it is and what it is used for: **"Look at the comb. We run a comb through our hair. Show me how to comb your hair."** If your baby needs help, take his hand. Close his fist as if he were holding a comb and then move his hand as if he were combing his hair: **"That's right. That's how to comb your hair."** The other family members should pantomime combing hair while your baby does.

Repeat the game using the other objects you've gathered. Give your baby help when needed. He may catch on by watching and imitating others pantomime. You may have a very busy evening as your family pretends to drink from a cup, brush their hair, throw a ball, eat from a spoon, read a book, and smell a flower! ✖

18. POP GOES THE WEASEL

Age Range
15-18 months

Materials
• None

When your family is together and needs to "burn off" some energy, try playing a simple circle game such as "Pop Goes the Weasel." It's a good game to try when you are looking for a quick way to entertain your baby. While playing the game with her family, she will also learn new words and coordinate the movements of her muscles.

To play the game, everyone must stand in a circle and join hands. Walk around in the circle as you sing the following song:

> *All around the mulberry bush,*
> *The monkey chased the weasel.*
> *The monkey thought it all in fun,*
> *Pop goes the weasel!*

You can perform one of several actions as you say "Pop." Everyone can bend at the waist and then straighten up. Or, if you feel more energetic, you can squat and then jump up. You may want to change the words in the last line to "Flop goes the weasel" and fall down as you say "Flop." Choose whichever version you think your baby (and family) would enjoy the most. Once you have chosen an ending, stick with it until your baby is a pro at it. If you

"Flop goes the weasel!"

try several different endings before she is familiar with one, it will probably confuse her.

If your baby enjoys "Pop Goes the Weasel," try other games such as "London Bridge" and "Ring Around the Rosie."

More About Small Wonder

Small Wonder is a two-level program of field-tested activities and support materials that stimulate the language development and the physical, emotional, and intellectual growth of babies and toddlers. It is used all over North America in day-care centers, preschool programs, parent-child centers, social service agency programs, home-based day care, special-education settings, pediatric centers, and homes. Level 1 is for babies from birth through 18 months; Level 2 continues with toddlers from 18 through 36 months. In addition to activity cards, each level includes a User's Guide, a puppet, picture cards, a plastic Look Book to display the picture cards, and a diary or progress chart. Level 2 also features a sound sheet containing original songs.

Small Wonder gets babies off to a good start! Delightfully inventive *Level 1* activities provide opportunities for the youngest children to strengthen muscle coordination, mimic sounds, explore their surroundings, learn to help themselves, follow simple directions, and begin to speak. Even daily routines such as bathing, diapering, dressing, and eating become special times to explore and learn when caregivers follow the clear directions given for each activity. These small wonders of accomplishment — shaking a rattle, recognizing a picture in a book, bouncing to a rhythm — are the beginning skills through which babies can learn and grow.

Lively *Level 2* activities stimulate toddlers' special readiness to speak and socialize and help satisfy children's need to start performing independently. Group games, outdoor activities, original songs, simple arts and crafts projects, and health and safety routines are presented in a fresh set of activities that give young children a sense of self-confidence and self-respect. Skills in problem solving, understanding abstract concepts, speech and language acquisition, toileting, and cooperation are some of the small wonders introduced in this new toddler program. *Level 2* follows as a developmentally sequenced continuation of *Level 1*, but it is wholly self-contained and may be used independently of the earlier program.

If you are a parent with a child in day care, find out whether your center is using *Small Wonder* and have them contact the publisher if they are not:

AGS
Publishers' Building
Circle Pines, MN 55014

If you are a professional care provider, write to AGS for a free, colorful brochure on the *Small Wonder* program. In Canada, contact Psycan, Ltd., 101 Amber Street, Markham, Ontario L3R 3B2.

Editorial Reviews
"*Small Wonder* for parents and caregivers to use with infants . . . is an activity program written in ordinary language and is aimed at both caregivers and parents. Karnes has an ability to summarize the key points of development and to describe these in a manner that is immediately understandable to anyone who has ever seen an infant.

"Considering Dr. Karnes' wealth of experience, it is not surprising to find that the activities are both carefully thought out and fun for the infant and caregiver.

More About Small Wonder

"A strength of the program throughout is the extent to which it helps the adult learn about infant development.

"*Small Wonder* . . . is developmentally sound, easy to follow and to implement, and does not require fancy or expensive extras . . . If you have infants in your center, you will want to explore *Small Wonder*."
Day Care and Early Education
Fall, 1979

"It has been a long time since I have seen material so well thought out. The pride and care in the production of the "*Small Wonder*" kit is obvious . . . it should be essential resource material in day cares, institutions for infants, parenting classes, child growth college classes and libraries. As a training guide for personnel who care for babies, it can't be beat at any price."
Southern Association on Children Under Six (SACUS)
Dimensions, April, 1980

Index of Activities According to Primary Skills Emphasized

This index lists the *Small Wonder* activities by skill category. Use it to locate activities emphasizing an aspect of development you want your baby to work on. Each category includes activities for children of different ages.

Balance and Motion Skills

Birth-3 Months
Lifting My Head (#2: *Just for the Two of You*)

3-6 Months
Looking Up (#4: *Chore-time Chums*)
Turning Toward the Source of a Sound (#5: *Chore-time Chums*)
Rolling Over (#5: *Just for the Two of You*)
Moving Around (#6: *A Classroom in the Kitchen*)

6-9 Months
Sitting Alone (#8: *Chore-time Chums*)
Moving Toward a Toy (#9: *Chore-time Chums*)
Pulling to a Stand (#9: *Just for the Two of You*)

9-12 Months
Crawling After "Wiggly" (#12: *Just for the Two of You*)

12-15 Months
Riding on a Towel (#13: *Just for the Fun of It*)
Riding on a Scooter (#13: *Growing with the Grass*)

Body Awareness

3-6 Months
Kicking a Toy (#4: *Just for the Fun of It*)

6-9 Months
Enjoying My Reflection in a Mirror (#7: *Just for the Fun of It*)

9-12 Months
Covering and Uncovering My Eyes (#11: *Changing Time*)
Looking at Myself (#11: *Chore-time Chums*)

12-15 Months
Discovering a Face (#15: *Changing Time*)
Blowing Bubbles (#15: *Bathtime Business*)

15-18 Months
Pointing to Body Parts (#17: *Bathtime Business*)

Cognitive Skills

Birth-3 Months
Touching (#3: *Changing Time*)

3-6 Months
Playing with Foil (#2: *Growing with the Grass*)
Discovering Animals (#2: *Shop, Look, and Listen*)
Feeling Textures (#5: *A Classroom in the Kitchen*)
Playing in the Stroller (#5: *Shop, Look, and Listen*)
Water Toys (#6: *Bathtime Business*)

6-9 Months
Looking at Bugs (#7: *Growing with the Grass*)
Exploring Objects (#7: *A Classroom in the Kitchen*)
Pouring from a Container (#9: *Just for the Fun of It*)
Playing with Water (#9: *Bathtime Business*)

9-12 Months
Exploring the Outdoors (#8: *Growing with the Grass*)
Bathtime Potpourri (#10: *Bathtime Business*)
Playing with Paper (#11: *Just for the Fun of It*)
Touring the House (#12: *Just for the Fun of It*)
Fun in the Kitchen Cabinet (#12: *A Classroom in the Kitchen*)
Hide-and-Seek with Objects (#12: *Chore-time Chums*)
Uncovering a Hidden Toy (#12: *Bathtime Business*)

12-15 Months
Smelling Spree (#11: *Shop, Look, and Listen*)
Playing a Game of "Checkers" (#14: *Just for the Two of You*)
Feats with Feet (#14: *Just for the Fun of It*)
Sniffing in the Kitchen (#15: *A Classroom in the Kitchen*)
Crawling Through a Tunnel (#15: *Chore-time Chums*)
Building with Blocks (#15: *Teaching — Family Style*)

15-18 Months
A Trip to a Hardware Store (#13: *Shop, Look, and Listen*)
Sidewalk Safety (#15: *Shop, Look, and Listen*)
Playing in the Sandbox (#16: *Just for the Fun of It*)
Nesting Bowls (#16: *A Classroom in the Kitchen*)
Pulling a String to Get a Toy (#17: *Just for the Fun of It*)
Solving Simple Problems (#18: *Just for the Two of You*)
Finger-Painting (#18: *Just for the Fun of It*)

Eating and Dressing Skills

6-9 Months
Feeding Myself (#7: *Teaching — Family Style*)

9-12 Months
Having a Picnic (#10: *Growing with the Grass*)

12-15 Months
Helping at Dressing Time (#14: *Changing Time*)

Index of Activities

15-18 Months
Brushing Hair (#17: *Changing Time*)
Getting Undressed (#18: *Bathtime Business*)

Exercise

Birth-3 Months
Bending and Stretching (#1: *Bathtime Business*)

3-6 Months
Going Up! (#4: *Changing Time*)
Exercising (#6: *Just for the Two of You*)
Exercising Legs (#6: *Teaching — Family Style*)

6-9 Months
Exercising in a Jumper Seat (#7: *Chore-time Chums*)
Exercising Arms and Legs (#8: *Just for the Two of You*)

Finger and Hand Skills

Birth-3 Months
Holding On (#2: *Changing Time*)

3-6 Months
Pulling (#4: *A Classroom in the Kitchen*)
Shaking a Rattle (#5: *Teaching — Family Style*)

6-9 Months
Handling Objects (#7: *Just for the Two of You*)
Tearing Paper (#7: *Changing Time*)
Picking Up and Dropping (#7: *Bathtime Business*)
Knocking Down a Tower (#8: *Bathtime Business*)
Stopping a Ball and Picking It Up (#8: *Teaching — Family Style*)
Hitting Pots and Pans (#9: *A Classroom in the Kitchen*)

9-12 Months
Stacking Bean Bags (#10: *Just for the Two of You*)
Magnets (#10: *A Classroom in the Kitchen*)
Removing Objects from a Container (#11: *A Classroom in the Kitchen*)
Putting Things into a Container (#11: *Bathtime Business*)

12-15 Months
Batting a Balloon (#13: *Teaching — Family Style*)
Dropping Objects into a Bottle (#14: *A Classroom in the Kitchen*)
Washing Hands (#14: *Bathtime Business*)

15-18 Months
Making a Nature Collage (#16: *Growing with the Grass*)

Language Development

Birth-3 Months
Looking and Listening (#2: *Chore-time Chums*)
A Little Conversation (#2: *Bathtime Business*)
Listening and Looking in the Kitchen (#3: *A Classroom in the Kitchen*)

3-6 Months
Imitating Sounds (#5: *Changing Time*)

6-9 Months
Stop and Go (#4: *Shop, Look, and Listen*)
Gesturing (#8: *Changing Time*)
Making Sounds (#8: *A Classroom in the Kitchen*)

9-12 Months
Handing Objects Back and Forth (#9: *Growing with the Grass*)

12-15 Months
Grocery-Store Games (#10: *Shop, Look, and Listen*)
Running Errands (#12: *Growing with the Grass*)
Learning New Words (#13: *A Classroom in the Kitchen*)
Learning to Follow Directions (#13: *Bathtime Business*)

15-18 Months
Understanding Simple Opposites (#16: *Changing Time*)
Selecting an Object (#16: *Bathtime Business*)
Naming Family Members in Photographs (#16: *Teaching — Family Style*)

Listening Skills

Birth-3 Months
Listening to a Song (#1: *A Classroom in the Kitchen*)
Listening to Kitchen Sounds (#2: *A Classroom in the Kitchen*)
Dancing with the Family (#2: *Teaching — Family Style*)
Listening (#3: *Just for the Fun of It*)

3-6 Months
The Check-out Counter (#3: *Shop, Look, and Listen*)
Listening to a Wind Chime (#4: *Growing with the Grass*)

6-9 Months
Outdoor Sounds (#5: *Growing with the Grass*)
Moving to Music (#8: *Just for the Fun of It*)

9-12 Months
A Trip to a Music Store (#9: *Shop, Look, and Listen*)

12-15 Months
Dancing Together (#13: *Just for the Two of You*)
Recognizing Sounds (#13: *Chore-time Chums*)
Family Song Time (#14: *Teaching — Family Style*)

Relaxation

Birth-3 Months
Enjoying a Massage (#1: *Just for the Two of You*)
Enjoying the Water (#3: *Bathtime Business*)

3-6 Months
Lying in the Tub (#4: *Bathtime Business*)
Enjoying a Back Massage (#5: *Bathtime Business*)

9-12 Months
Leg and Foot Massage (#10: *Changing Time*)

Socialization Skills

Birth-3 Months
Mealtime (#1: *Teaching — Family Style*)
Smiling at Faces (#3: *Teaching — Family Style*)

3-6 Months
Playing Rhyme Games (#4: *Just for the Two of You*)
Enjoying Others (#4: *Teaching — Family Style*)
Playing Peek-a-Boo (#6: *Changing Time*)
The Playpen (#6: *Chore-time Chums*)

6-9 Months
Meeting New People (#6: *Growing with the Grass*)
Learning Hand Movements for a Song (#9: *Changing Time*)

9-12 Months
Playing "Catch Me" (#10: *Just for the Fun of It*)
Peek-a-Boo (#10: *Chore-time Chums*)
Two Games for Two People (#11: *Just for the Two of You*)
Getting Acquainted with Another Baby (#11: *Growing with the Grass*)
Changing-Time Rhymes (#12: *Changing Time*)
Retrieving Bean Bags (#12: *Teaching — Family Style*)

12-15 Months
Sharing Food (#12: *Shop, Look, and Listen*)
Hanging Up My Clothes (#13: *Changing Time*)
Playing Catch (#14: *Chore-time Chums*)
Touch the Light (#15: *Just for the Fun of It*)

15-18 Months
Eating in a Restaurant (#14: *Shop, Look, and Listen*)
Swimming Pool Fun (#15: *Growing with the Grass*)
Pretending to Talk on the Telephone (#16: *Just for the Two of You*)
Fixing Dinner (#17: *A Classroom in the Kitchen*)
Dusting (#17: *Chore-time Chums*)
Pantomiming: (#17: *Teaching — Family Style*)
Setting the Table (#18: *A Classroom in the Kitchen*)
Putting Away Toys (#18: *Chore-time Chums*)
Pop Goes the Weasel (#18: *Teaching — Family Style*)

Visual Skills

Birth-3 Months
Watching Movement (#1: *Just for the Fun of It*)
Taking a Look (#1: *Changing Time*)
Looking Around Outdoors (#1: *Growing with the Grass*)
Looking at Lights (#1: *Chore-time Chums*)
Looking Around at the Store (#1: *Shop, Look, and Listen*)
Looking in a Mirror Alone (#2: *Just for the Fun of It*)
Looking Around (#3: *Just for the Two of You*)
Cradle Gym (#3: *Chore-time Chums*)

3-6 Months
Studying Nature (#3: *Growing with the Grass*)
Looking in a Mirror Together (#5: *Just for the Fun of It*)
Looking at What I'm Holding (#6: *Just for the Fun of It*)

6-9 Months
Examining Objects (#6: *Shop, Look, and Listen*)
Looking at a Book (#9: *Teaching — Family Style*)

9-12 Months
Entertaining in the Car (#7: *Shop, Look, and Listen*)
A Trip to a Fabric Store (#8: *Shop, Look, and Listen*)
Watching a Puppet Show (#10: *Teaching — Family Style*)
Follow the Leader (#11: *Teaching — Family Style*)

12-15 Months
Looking at Photographs of Baby (#15: *Just for the Two of You*)

15-18 Months
Matching Objects and Pictures (#14: *Growing with the Grass*)
Matching Socks (#16: *Chore-time Chums*)
Enjoying a Book (#17: *Just for the Two of You*)

More Parenting Books from AGS

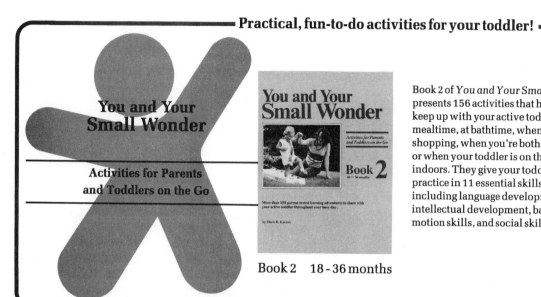